Better Homes and Gardens®

DO·IT·YOURSELF

WIRING

D1304648

Excerpted from Better Homes and Gardens®
Complete Guide to Home Repair, Maintenance, and Improvement
© Copyright 1989 by Meredith Corporation, Des Moines, Iowa.
All Rights Reserved. Printed in the United States of America.
First Edition. Second Printing, 1989.
ISBN: 0-696-01867-5

INTRODUCTION

Electricity helps keep your home secure, convenient, and comfortable. With a little knowledge of home wiring, you can make its energy serve you even better. You can add outlets, switches, and light fixtures where you need them; safeguard your family against electrical hazards; and run new circuits to underpowered areas of your home. Even if you're a novice at working with electricity, Better Homes and Gardens® *Do-It-Yourself Wiring* will help you master the techniques you need to know to safely do these and many other jobs. With hundreds of concise, easy-to-follow illustrations, *Do-It-Yourself Wiring* gives you the information—and the confidence—you need to build your skills.

BETTER HOMES AND GARDENS® BOOKS
Editor: Gerald M. Knox
Art Director: Ernest Shelton
Managing Editor: David A. Kirchner
Editorial Project Managers: Liz Anderson, James D. Blume,
  Marsha Jahns

Do-It-Yourself Wiring
Editors: Gayle Goodson Butler and James A. Hufnagel
Editorial Project Manager: Liz Anderson
Electronic Text Processor: Paula Forest

Complete Guide to Home Repair, Maintenance and Improvement
Project Editors: Larry Clayton, Noel Seney
Research and Writing: James A. Hufnagel
Graphic Designer: Richard Lewis
Illustrations: Graphic Center

CONTENTS

ELECTRICITY

To most people, a household electrical system seems mysterious and even dangerous. Actually, its principles rest on elementary logic. Master them, observe a few precautions that will soon become second nature, and you can safely pull off a wide variety of electrical repair and improvement jobs.

Let's take a quick look at the overall system that keeps you comfortably supplied with electricity. Power from the utility comes in through a *service entrance*—either in overhead or underground wires—to a *meter* that keeps track of your household's consumption. Then the power continues on to a *service panel* that breaks it down into a series of *circuits*. These circuits deliver current throughout the house. *Fuses* or *circuit breakers* at the service panel control individual circuits and protect against fire, which could develop if a circuit draws more current than it's designed to handle.

GETTING TO KNOW YOUR SYSTEM

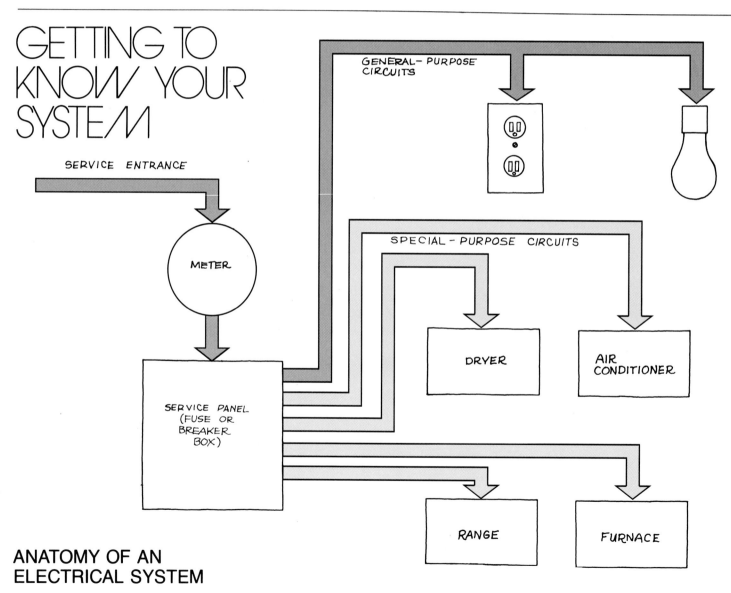

SERVICE ENTRANCE

GENERAL-PURPOSE CIRCUITS

METER

SPECIAL-PURPOSE CIRCUITS

SERVICE PANEL (FUSE OR BREAKER BOX)

DRYER

AIR CONDITIONER

RANGE

FURNACE

ANATOMY OF AN ELECTRICAL SYSTEM

UNDERSTANDING ELECTRICAL TERMINOLOGY

Electrical *current* flows—under pressure—through the wiring in your house. That flow would come to an absolute halt if you were to disconnect every single appliance, light, and other device you have. But as soon as you start up one "customer," the flow in that particular circuit begins.

The amount of current (measured in *amps*) going through a wire at a given time is based on the number of electrons passing a certain point each second. The pressure that forces these electrons along their route is known as *voltage* (measured in *volts*).

If you were to increase the voltage, you would not accelerate the flow of current; current travels at a constant speed—the speed of light. But you would increase the *power* in your lines; that power is measured in *watts* and is the product you get when you multiply amps times volts. Your utility bills, incidentally, are based on the number of watts—in thousands—you consume each hour. The common term is *kilowatt-hour.*

When current flows to a plug outlet, for example, the electrons travel inside what's called a *hot wire,* which is black (or, in rare cases, a white wire with black paint or tape to indicate that it's functioning as a hot wire). After current has flowed through a light or appliance, the electrons seek a direct route to *ground* (see page 9) and travel in white *neutral* wires to get there. These neutrals, also known as *system grounds,* complete every circuit in the system by returning its current to the ground.

Modern circuits have three wires, the third being a bare or green one that serves as an *equipment ground.* Its role is to ground all metal parts throughout your installation, such as conduit, armored cable, motors, and major appliances. This grounding wire protects against the danger of short circuits.

COMPLYING WITH CODES AND INSPECTIONS

The National Electrical Code, published every three years by the National Fire Protection Association, is the most complete, detailed set of guidelines you're apt to find anywhere. So, if you're planning any major wiring job, get hold of a copy; the book is full of helpful tips. But despite the Code's strong influence nationally, the last word on what you can and can't do electrically comes from your local building code. Its provisions are law and take precedence over anything you'll see in the national code.

A few localities won't even allow do-it-yourselfers to work on their own wiring; others make you get a temporary permit first. Some areas permit homeowners to undertake all but the final connection at the service entrance panel, so be sure to check with the building department in your community to find out what's in store for you. And, of course, expect to arrange to have your work inspected at the end of the project.

HOW TO READ YOUR METER

Though you'll occasionally see a meter that looks like a car odometer, most types have a series of four or five dials. The leftmost dial indicates tens of thousands of kilowatt-hours; the next one to the right, thousands; and so on.

Read the leftmost dial first, then proceed to the right. When a pointer is between two digits, always read the lower number. If the pointer is right on a number, read the next lower number only if the dial to the right has not yet passed the zero mark.

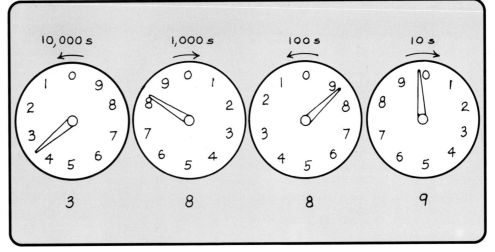

CHECKING OUT YOUR SERVICE PANEL

Circuit Breaker Panels

Most electrical projects begin at the service panel—also called a *breaker box* or *fuse box*. It's the heart of your system and home base for protective devices that automatically disconnect power to the entire house or to individual branch circuits in case of overloads or shorts. The panel also is the place you go to shut off the current manually when you want to work on a circuit or two.

In most newer installations, the safety devices protecting you are called *circuit breakers*. The typical service box (at right) will have one main cutoff breaker and several smaller breakers, each controlling its own branch circuit. After you find and correct the problem, reset the breaker by flipping the toggle switch to its *on* position.

Unlike the switch-type breakers. this style has a button that you push in to turn off power. push in again to restore it.

Fuse Boxes

If you have an older home in which the original wiring is intact, chances are your service panel contains fuses rather than breakers. And instead of "tripping," which is what breakers do when problems occur, fuses "blow." Whenever the current builds up beyond the level intended for a particular circuit and its fuse, the thin strip of metal that carries the current through the fuse simply melts in a flash. As soon as this happens, the circuit is open, and current flow comes to a screeching halt.

Usually, you'll find a main pullout block with two cartridge-type fuses (see next page) mounted on its backside. Just grab the handle, pull out the block, and you'll shut off the entire house. (Some older boxes have a shutoff lever.) Most smaller branch circuits are protected by another kind of fuse—usually a screw-in plug fuse rated at 15 or 20 amps.

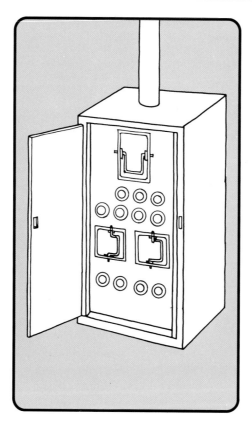

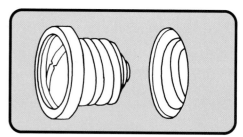

A plug fuse. threaded like a light bulb. screws into the fuse box. Handle only the rim when replacing this type of fuse.

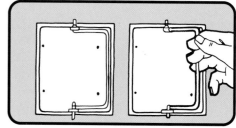

Larger 240-volt circuits for water heaters and the like generally are protected by small pullout blocks with cartridge fuses.

TYPES OF FUSES

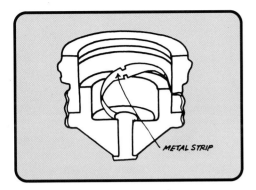

With the most common variety, the *plug fuse*, a metal strip melts and breaks the circuit in case of shorts or overloads.

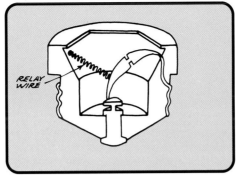

Use *time-delay* fuses for circuits that overload for just a few seconds. The fuse blows only for shorts or continuous overloads.

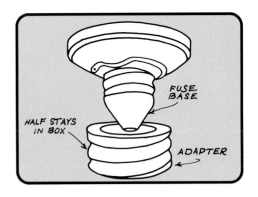

The bases of *Type-S* fuses are sized by amp rating. Adapters installed permanently in the box accept only matching fuse bases.

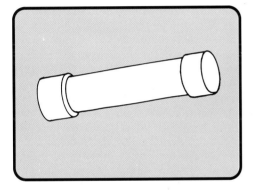

For circuits larger than 30 amps, use one of two types of cartridge fuses. The *ferrule-contact* style comes in sizes through 60 amps.

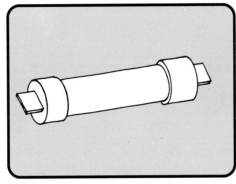

Knife-blade-contact fuses are rated higher than 60 amps. Both types of cartridge fuses can have time-delay features.

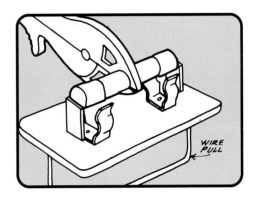

Use a plastic *fuse puller* to remove a cartridge fuse from an auxiliary fuse box or from the back of a pullout block.

HOW TO "READ" A BLOWN FUSE

Diagnosing the cause of a blown fuse is easy, mainly because the culprit usually leaves a telltale sign behind. An ordinary plug fuse will have a blackened window if a short has occurred. And in case of an overload, the metal strip will separate (see drawings at right). Time-delay fuses react the same way to shorts as do plug fuses. But if an overload hits a time-delay model, solder in the bottom of the fuse loosens and releases a metal strip that is pulled upward by a coiled wire.

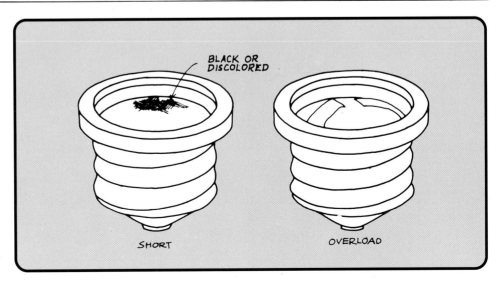

SOLVING ELECTRICAL PROBLEMS

HOW'S YOUR HOUSE POWER?

Has your electrical system kept up with the demands placed on it by all the new work-savers you've accumulated recently? Chances are, it hasn't. A 100-amp service used to be more than enough for most homes. But today, you're likely to need 150 or 200 amps.

If a constant harassment of overloads keeps you busy changing fuses (or resetting breakers) and juggling appliances from one plug outlet to another, you already know you have a problem. Here's a scientific way to track it down.

Because circuits are rated at the service panel in terms of amps, you'll have to do some elementary arithmetic to get an amp rating for every electrical "customer" in your house. But before you start calculating, you'll need to take a complete survey of your house, listing every electrical appliance and device by circuit. (When you're through, post a duplicate of that rundown next to—or inside the door of—your service panel. It can tell you at a glance which fuse to pull or breaker to flip when you want to work on a specific outlet or switch.)

Now, using the formula amps = watts ÷ volts, you can figure the amperage requirements of each electrical device on each circuit. Most of your circuits are 120 volts, and you should be able to find either a wattage figure or amperage figure for every bulb, appliance, and other electrical item you have. If you're lucky enough to find an amp figure, you're already there. And if you come up with a wattage figure, just divide it by 120 to determine the amperage.

The last step, of course, is to add up all of the amperage figures for each circuit and compare that total with the amperage capacity appearing on the appropriate breaker or fuse. Now you'll know for sure if that circuit would face an overload if every customer tied into it called for current at the same time.

If your survey turns up some nerve-jangling match-ups, you should add circuits, shuffle outlets from one circuit to another, or do a little of both.

As you can see from the sketch below, so-called general-purpose circuits need 15-amp breakers or fuses, whereas the special-purpose circuits serving large appliances require greater capacities. In addition to the circuits depicted below, you should have at least two 20-amp small-appliance circuits in the kitchen. Also supply your workshop with its own—or a lightly used—20-amp circuit.

Individual 240-volt circuits are in order for central air conditioners, electric ranges, electric dryers, electric water heaters, electric furnaces, and heat pumps.

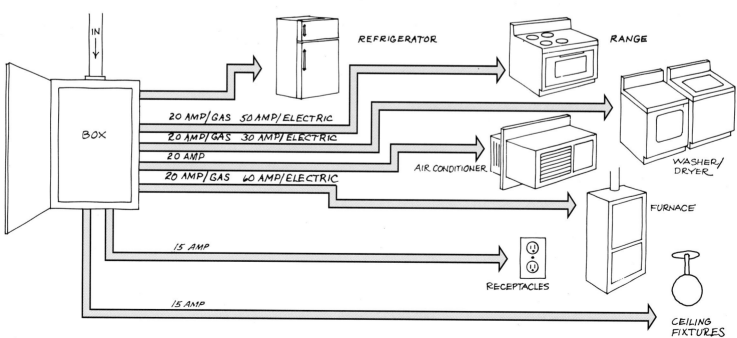

IS YOUR ENTIRE INSTALLATION GROUNDED?

If you've ever stood on a wet basement floor and been jolted with a good, strong electrical shock, you've participated in a live demonstration of how electrical current seeks the shortest route to the ground. That time, it used you as its conductor; wire is a much more comfortable vehicle. When a short crops up in your wiring or in a device connected to it, your best protection is a properly grounded circuit.

There are several bits of background information you should know in order to minimize the chance of shock and electrical fire, and even damage from lightning. First, let's distinguish between two different kinds of grounding. *System grounding* is the grounding of current-carrying wires. *Equipment grounding* is the grounding of non-current-carrying portions of your wiring installation, such as the frames of motors and appliances, as well as smaller metal items, such as conduit, armored (BX) cable, and boxes for fixtures, switches, and receptacles.

Proper grounding starts in the service panel at the *grounding bus bar,* which is connected—literally—to earth by a cable (known as the *ground wire*). This is fastened either to a metal rod driven into the earth outside your house or to your incoming water-supply pipe. The bus bar, in turn, has solderless connectors or screw terminals to which two other types of wires are connected—*grounded wires* and *grounding wires.*

Grounded wires are the white neutral wires that complete each of your circuits by returning current to its source, and in so doing, ground the *system.* (Also connected to the bus bar is the incoming neutral wire from the utility company.) Grounding wires—usually bare, green, or green with yellow stripes—are the ones that ground the *equipment.*

One example will explain why it's so important to have an equipment ground. If a short circuit should crop up inside a motor, there's a chance the motor would still run and that the fuse or breaker wouldn't react. The frame of the motor could then become "live," and anyone touching the live frame could complete the circuit through his or her body into the ground. A properly installed grounding wire would have routed that errant current safely back through the bus bar and into the ground.

There are two basic ways to obtain a good equipment ground, depending on the type of wiring you have. For circuits with individual wires strung inside metal conduit or armored (BX) cable, the conduit or cable must be mechanically connected to each box and to the service panel. A tight connection ensures proper grounding. Where nonmetallic-sheathed cable is used, the cable must contain three wires—a hot, a neutral, and a bare grounding wire. The grounding wire must extend from the metal switch or outlet box to the bus bar. In many older homes, neither of these situations exists.

The bare equipment-grounding wires and the white system-grounding neutrals connect to terminals on the bus bar.

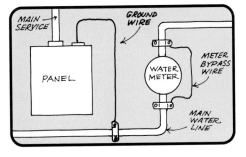

When using the water-supply pipe for a ground, add a bypass to keep the grounding complete in case the meter is removed.

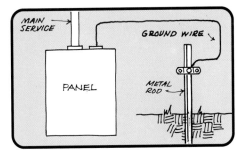

The alternative to using a water pipe as a ground is to attach the ground wire to a metal rod that's been driven into the earth.

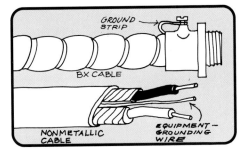

Shown here are two equipment grounds. The BX cable makes metal-to-metal contact; its ground strip adds extra insurance.

A two-prong adapter is grounded only if the screw that holds the pigtail is in contact with a properly grounded outlet box.

TOOLS FOR ELECTRICAL REPAIRS

You probably already have on hand a good number of the tools you'll need for electrical work—old standbys such as a hammer, drill, keyhole saw, chisel, screwdrivers, hacksaw, measuring tape, and the like. But there are a few special-purpose tools you'll want to buy, rent, or borrow before you take on an electrical project of any size. And if you decide to buy them, choose only quality tools. They'll work better and last much longer than their bargain-basket look-alikes.

The examples below represent the bulk of the tools you'll need to solve the electrical problems treated on the next four pages. To learn about a few more items necessary for bigger jobs, see page 20.

The *fish tape* can be bought with or without a reel. The two *testers* are musts and are described on the next page.

Some electricians like to use the *combination tool* because it can both cut and strip wire and crimp special fasteners, whereas others prefer to stick with the simpler *wire stripper*. You'll use the *side-cutting pliers* to snip wires in tough-to-reach places, and *lineman's pliers* have heavy square jaws that are ideal for twisting wires together. *Long-nose pliers* make quick work of curling loops on the ends of wires.

Also round up a sharp straight-bladed pocketknife or a *utility knife* to slit the sheathing lengthwise on nonmetallic cable. Use a *nut driver* to reach into places wrenches can't touch. And collect a good assortment of *wire nuts* in various sizes to help you make quick wire-to-wire connections.

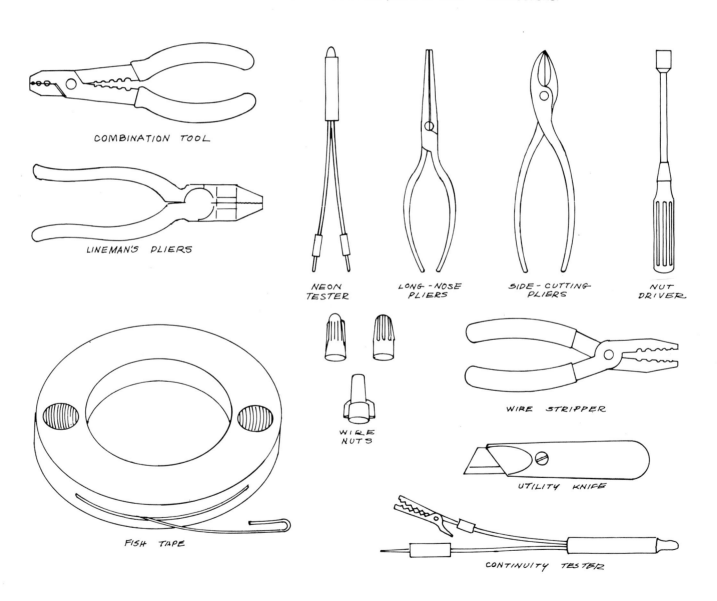

COMBINATION TOOL

LINEMAN'S PLIERS

NEON TESTER

LONG-NOSE PLIERS

SIDE-CUTTING PLIERS

NUT DRIVER

WIRE NUTS

WIRE STRIPPER

FISH TAPE

UTILITY KNIFE

CONTINUITY TESTER

TESTING CIRCUITS

There's a certain amount of detective work to be done when making electrical repairs (or improvements). That sleuthing is made much easier by the two testers shown here. You'll use the neon type mainly when the current is on, usually to find out if power is present at switches, lights, and receptacles.

Continuity testers, on the other hand, are used only with the power turned off. They have their own power source and are just the thing to test a switch, socket, cartridge fuse, etc.

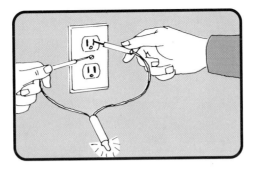

If the neon tester lights up when touched to a receptacle box as shown, the plate screw is properly grounded.

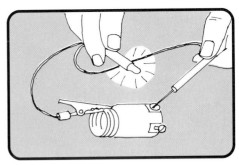

A lamp socket checks out OK if the continuity tester lights up when the alligator clip and probe are placed as shown.

MAKING CONNECTIONS

Whether you're joining wires to switches, receptacles, or in mid-circuit, for safety's sake make all connections inside a box. At switches and receptacles, you'll run into one of two types of terminals—screws and grip holes. The screw type is self-explanatory; you simply loosen the screw, strip and curl the end of the wire, and place the loop around the screw—clockwise. Then securely tighten the screw.

The devices that come with grip holes can be wired in a jiffy. After you've stripped the wire, just shove it into the appropriate slot where a locking piece will grab the wire tightly. If you ever want to remove the wire for any reason, press a small screwdriver against a release slot marked on the device, and the wire will slip out.

Solderless connectors (wire nuts) make a simple job of joining wires. See details below.

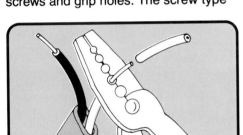

Remove the insulation—usually about ¾ inch—from each wire with a stripper. Wire size is indicated alongside each hole.

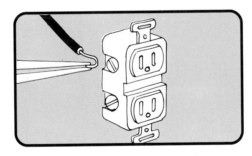

Use long-nose pliers to bend the end of the wire into a loop to curl around the shank of the terminal screw.

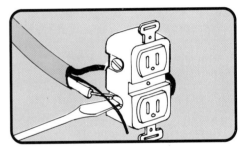

Be sure the screws are tight—but not too tight. An overzealous twist of the screwdriver can crack the plastic body.

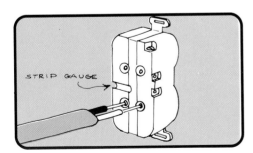

Devices with grip holes have a strip gauge marked on them to show you exactly how much insulation to remove.

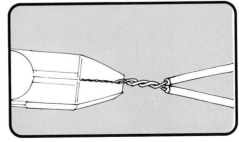

To ensure a solid connection when you use wire nuts, first strip the wires and twist them together with a lineman's pliers.

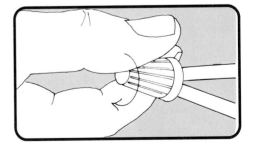

Shove the wire nut tightly against the wires as you turn it clockwise as far as it will go. Be sure no bare wire is exposed.

TROUBLESHOOTING LAMPS

A table lamp is one of the simplest examples of electricity at work . . . and one of the easiest projects to troubleshoot. Whenever the bulb in one of your lamps won't light, the first thing to check is the bulb. If a new one won't work, the next place to look is the receptacle. The easiest way to find out if it's hot is to plug in another lamp. If it works, you've narrowed down the problem to one of three remaining areas—the plug, the cord, or the socket. Then check the table at right.

Symptom	Cause	Cure
Won't light	Loose connection Broken wire	Tighten connection Replace cord
Blows fuse	Frayed cord Defective plug Defective socket	Tape or replace cord Replace plug Replace socket
Light flickers	Loose connection Defective switch	Tighten connection Replace switch

REPLACING A LAMP CORD

Cracked or worn lamp cords not only can cause a serious shock, they're also fire hazards. So why take a chance! Make the repair as soon as you spot trouble. And while you're at it, replace the old socket as well.

The easiest way to install the new cord is to tie a string between it and the old one so that new can follow old up through the lamp's base.

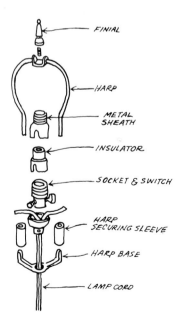

- FINIAL
- HARP
- METAL SHEATH
- INSULATOR
- SOCKET & SWITCH
- HARP SECURING SLEEVE
- HARP BASE
- LAMP CORD

To expose the socket. push hard on the outer shell where it says "PRESS" and pull off the shell and insulating jacket.

Loosen the terminal screws. remove the old cord (install the new one simultaneously). and tie an Underwriter's knot as shown.

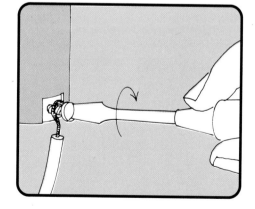

Twist the braided strands tightly. curl them as shown. and screw one wire to each terminal in a clockwise direction.

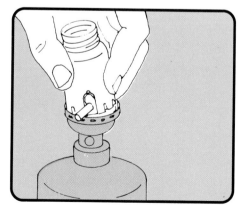

Gently pull the wire from below to draw the socket against its base. then replace the insulating and outer shells.

REPLACING PLUGS

If you find a plug with loose prongs, a cracked body, or a blackened spot (evidence of a short), replace it pronto—the expense is minimal, and the work is a breeze. Even if you don't see any obvious signs of problems, you might as well change the plug if you're replacing a worn cord—they're most likely of the same vintage.

You'll normally run into two types of plugs—some for round cords and others for flat cords. Vacuum cleaners, irons, and the like usually have a round-cord plug; flat-cord plugs come with lower-amperage appliances such as radios, clocks, and lamps. Be sure your replacement plug is the same basic type as the original.

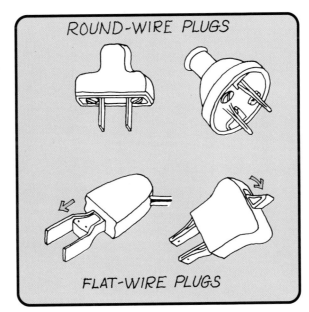

The two top plugs, designed for round wires, are hooked up as shown below. The other two accommodate a flat wire known as *zip cord,* the type widely used for lamp repairs. It consists of two conductors connected by a thin membrane that you can tear easily when you want to separate the wires.

To wire these plugs, insert the squared-off end of the zip cord into a slot and depress a lever (or push two parts together). Internal prongs penetrate the insulation and complete the circuit.

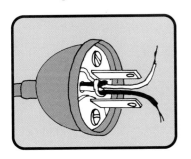

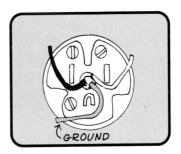

Remove the outer sheath, insert the cord, and tie the Underwriter's knot (see opposite). Then strip insulation from both wires.

Tightly twist the strands of each wire, loop each clockwise around a screw, then carefully tighten the screws. Tuck in stray strands.

With grounded plugs, insert the cord and tie together all three wires. Then pull the knot down snugly into the plug.

Strip insulation, twist strands to firm up wire, then loop and fasten under screws. Replace the protective insulating cover.

CHOOSING EXTENSION CORDS

You can usually get by with a few 10-amp two-wire extension cords. But it's better to have at least one larger capacity cord—say, a 20-amp size—for hooking up appliances that draw more current than a radio or vacuum cleaner. For your workshop, you'll want a large-capacity three-wire cord—usually with No. 14 wire—to handle your power tools.

The longer the cord, the greater the chance of a current drop, so use the shortest cord possible. Check the table at right for buying guidelines.

Use	Length	Size
Lamps, clocks, etc. to 7 amps	To 25 ft.	No. 18
	To 50 ft.	No. 16
	To 100 ft.	No. 14
Small appliances, etc. to 10 amps	To 25 ft.	No. 16
	To 50 ft.	No. 14
	To 100 ft.	No. 12
Large appliances, power tools	To 25 ft.	No. 14
	To 50 ft.	No. 12
	To 100 ft.	No. 10
Note: The larger the wire number, the smaller the wire's size.		

REPLACING RECEPTACLES

If a receptacle goes bad and you're elected to replace it, you won't need a cram course in wiring theory. The job's already done for you. All you need to do is wire the new outlet exactly as the old one was done. Note: in newer homes and some older ones, there's often a (third) ground wire, which connects to the receptacle. This is an equipment ground wire. See page 9 for more information on grounding.

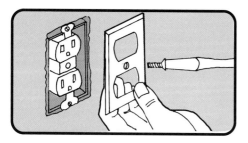

Before you start. remember to turn off the power at the main disconnect or circuit breaker. Then remove the faceplate.

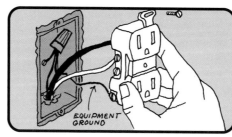

Remove the screws fastening the receptacle to the box at top and bottom. and pull the receptacle from the box.

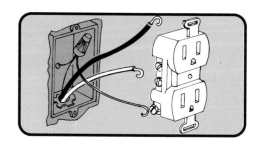

Before you disconnect anything. make a quick sketch to help you remember where each wire goes. Then remove the wires.

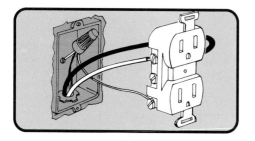

Hook up the new receptacle. using your sketch if needed. Test your handiwork by restoring power to the receptacle.

Working on a side-by-side installation is just as easy as a single receptacle. Just remember to sketch the wiring layout.

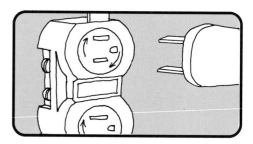

If you have small children. consider using child-proof safety receptacles. You have to twist a cover to expose the slots.

REPLACING SWITCHES

Whether you're replacing a switch because it's bad or just because you want a different style, the job shouldn't take longer than 15 minutes. And that includes a couple minutes to go to the service panel and cut the power to the circuit you're working on.

The common household switch is a *single-pole* variety that has two brass-colored terminals and—in some cases—a grounding terminal. (Some brands come with grip holes instead of screws.) A switch is wired only into the hot line, with the *source feed* usually connected to the top terminal.

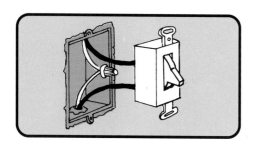

The neutral wires in this circuit are independent of the switch and continue all the way back to the service panel.

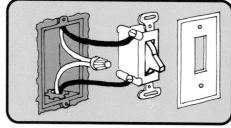

You won't always find the terminals on your new switch positioned the same as on the old one. Here they face the side.

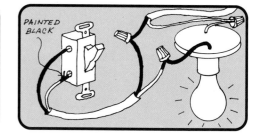

In this exception to the color rules. the white wire in the cable is painted black to indicate that it's serving as a hot wire.

RUNNING NEW WIRING

Extending an existing circuit or adding a new one calls more for careful thinking than for actual skill or hard work. Most components fasten together surprisingly easily, so your hardest task will be to become familiar with the vast array of electrical materials on the market. A good way to start is to visit a well-stocked electrical supply house and take a long, detailed look at the products on display. Try to figure out for yourself how one component ties into another. If you're stumped, ask someone for help.

Then tour a home under construction that's still at the wiring stage. There—all exposed for you—is the whole story, from panel to light switch and all points in between. Take notes, make diagrams, pay attention to details, and digest what you see.

WIRE SIZES

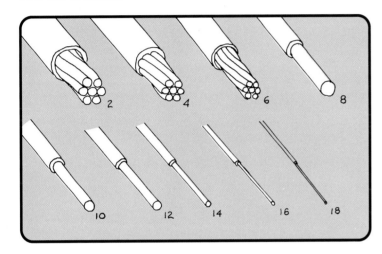

Though all of the wires above (about actual size) are used in homes. you're most likely to work with No. 14 and No. 12.

The smaller sizes (Nos. 16 and 18) are used mainly for doorbells and other installations involving small currents.

WIRE COVERINGS

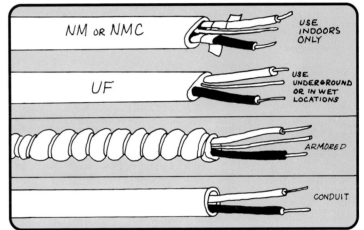

Nonmetallic sheathed cable is inexpensive and easy to work with. Use Type NM in dry places. NMC in wet areas. UF underground.

Steel armored cable is flexible and protects wiring from damage. Conduit. though rigid, can be bent with a special tool.

HOW TO "READ" A CABLE

Codes specify the type and sizes of cable you may install. For indoor use, most permit Type NM, shown at right. Its outer sheath is usually a moisture-resistant, flame-retardant plastic that's soft and easy to strip away to get to the wires. You'll find two or three insulated conductors (wires) inside. If two, one will be black, the other white; if three, you'll see a red one in there, too. In addition to the insulated wires, you may find a bare one—the equipment ground.

The markings at right tell you that the cable contains two No. 14 insulated conductors and a grounding wire.

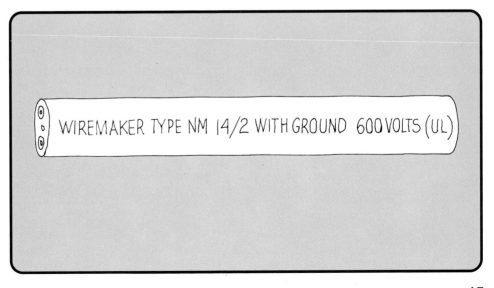

WIREMAKER TYPE NM 14/2 WITH GROUND 600 VOLTS (UL)

15

WORKING WITH WIRE

Both nonmetallic sheathed cable and armored cable come with the wires already inside. And though the sheathed type is easier to work with, you may be required by local codes to use the armored variety.

Most often, either of these is concealed within walls where it runs little risk of being damaged. Run it vertically between the studs or horizontally through holes drilled in the studs. (Be sure the holes are at least 1½ inches from the front of the stud.)

When you buy armored cable, stock up on anti-short bushings; these prevent the cable's sharp edges from damaging the wires' insulation.

Sheathed Cable

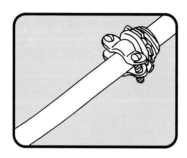

To tie sheathed cable into a box. first slip a box connector about seven inches onto the cable and tighten the screws.

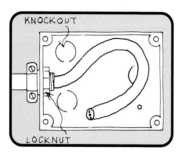

Remove a knockout from the side of the box and insert the threaded end of the connector. Then screw on the locknut.

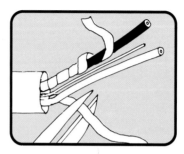

After the cable is anchored to the box. slit and remove the outer sheath and cut away the spiraled layer of kraft paper.

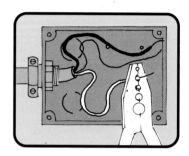

Now use a wire stripper (match hole size to wire gauge) to remove about ¾ inch of insulation from both conductors.

Armored (BX) Cable

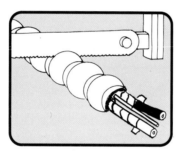

Partially cut armored cable—at an angle—with a hacksaw. Be careful not to nick the insulation on the wires.

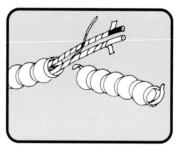

Twist the cut end and pull it off. Unwind the kraft paper as far as you can. then give it a quick. hard jerk to tear it free.

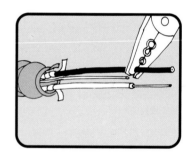

Next. strip both wires back about ¾ inch. You'll find a wire stripper the best tool for this. but you also can use a knife.

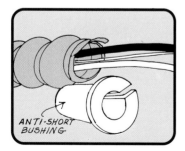

Because the cut edges of the steel armor are rough, you're required to insert an anti-short bushing to protect the wires.

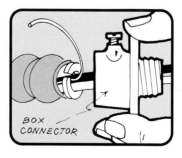

Fold back the ground strip. then shove a special box connector firmly onto the cable as far as it will go. Check for sharp edges.

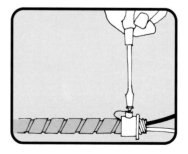

Wrap the ground strip around the screw on top of the connector and tighten the screw firmly with a screwdriver.

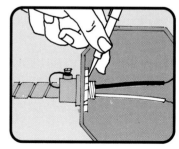

Remove a knockout. insert the connector. and screw on the locknut. Then pound a nail set against the lugs to tighten the nut.

WORKING WITH CONDUIT

As mentioned earlier, unprotected electrical cable—unless it's tucked safely inside a wall, floor, or ceiling—is susceptible to damage. So whenever you're running wiring in an unfinished basement or garage, or for any special situation, protect yourself and your wiring with metal conduit.

Though there are four types of conduit available, you'll probably encounter only the *thin-wall* type (formerly called *electrical metallic tubing* in the Code). It's sold in 10-foot lengths that you can join end to end with fittings called *couplings* and to boxes with *connectors.* Various types of these are shown below.

The trickiest part of working with conduit comes when you must bend it to get around corners or make the small offsets necessary at each box. To do this, you slip the conduit into a bender, as illustrated, then gently lever the bender toward you. Make a bend gradually, with a series of tugs along its radius. Pull too sharply at any one point and you'll crimp the tubing.

The importance of making smooth bends (and a minimum of them) becomes clear after you've installed a run of conduit and fitted boxes at either end. Now it's time to pull wires through the installation. Too many bends—and any crimps at all—will hang up the wires, and you risk damaging their insulation when you pull.

Limit bends in any run between boxes to a total of 360 degrees. If an installation will traverse more than the equivalent of four quarter-bends, install an additional box.

Most codes specify that you use *Type TW* wires within conduit. Since each of these conductors is separately insulated, you'll need at least two (one black, one white) for each run. To pull the wires, first thread a fish tape through the tubing and attach the wires to it as shown below and on page 22. Never splice wires within conduit—a poorly made connection here could make the entire run "live."

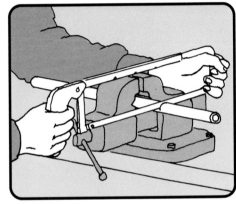

Bend conduit first, then cut it to length. You'll probably need to make a few practice bends before you master this knack.

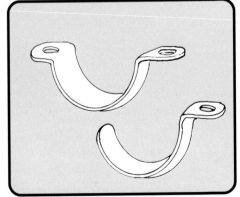

Use a vise to hold the conduit while you cut it to size with a hacksaw. File off the burrs to prevent damaging the wiring.

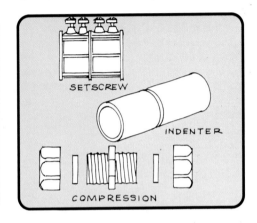

Shown are the three types of commonly used conduit couplings. The *indenter* version requires a special crimping tool.

Three main varieties of box connectors, which match the three couplings described above, secure the conduit safely in place.

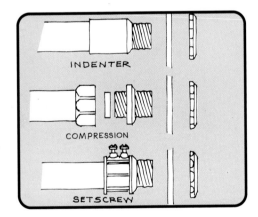

Anchor ½-inch thin-wall conduit to the wall or ceiling with one- or two-hole clamps near boxes and at least every ten feet.

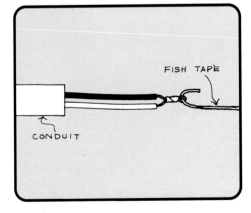

In short runs, you usually can push wires through conduit. On longer runs, pull the wires with a spring-steel fish tape.

USING
SURFACE WIRING

Metal Raceway

Surface metal raceways allow you an alternate method of adding circuits to your electrical system. Instead of tearing into walls and working in tight places, you install this product out in the open, usually along or near the baseboard.

Both commonly available types of raceway, the one-piece and the two-piece, install easily. The one-piece, which is simply a channel, attaches to the wall with couplings, clips, and straps. After you've mounted the hardware, you pull the wiring through the channels and make your connections. A host of fittings is available to help you build a raceway network suited to your particular needs. In a two-piece system, you mount the back to the wall, lay your wiring inside the cover, then snap the cover onto the back.

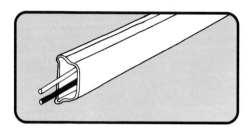

For safety reasons. one-piece raceway must be exposed. except when it runs through a wall to continue into the next room.

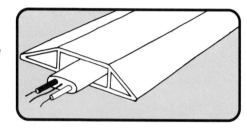

There's even a one-piece "pan-cake" channel available for installations that require running wiring on top of the floor.

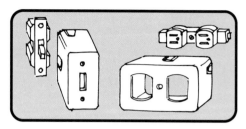

All types of elbows. T-connectors. reducing connectors—even receptacles and switches—tie into modular raceway systems.

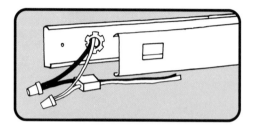

For two-piece raceway. you don't need a wall box. Power enters via cable connected to the wall-mounted backing plate.

WHAT'S AVAILABLE
IN BOXES AND
ACCESSORIES

For Exposed Walls

Because all switches, receptacles, fixtures (except fluorescents), and junctions must be protected by a box, you can appreciate why there are hundreds of different boxes on the market.

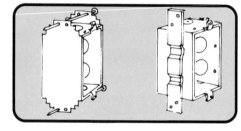

You can nail either of these boxes to the side of a stud. The one at left has its own 16d nails; a bracket is attached to the other.

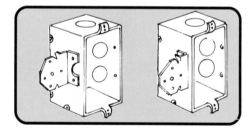

These boxes nail to the front of a stud. The brackets are recessed to allow for the thickness of the wall surface being applied.

For Finished Walls

If you're faced with installing a box in a wall that's already finished off, the job's a little more complicated. But the toughest part of it is cutting the hole and fishing the wires—not mounting the box.

Fortunately, the products at right make the box-installation step a fairly simple process—even for beginners. Before you begin, you might want to consult a carpentry manual for information about cutting different wall materials.

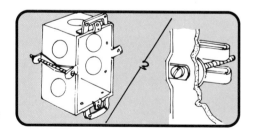

Shove this box into the opening till the ears stop it. Then turn the two clamp screws to tighten the box against the wall.

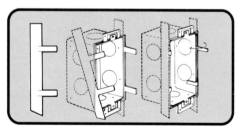

With this type. you slip flat metal box supports alongside the box. then fold the tabs into the box to snug it against the wall.

The Basic Box

You'll get a lot of mileage out of this box, especially if you use the style that comes with internal clamps. (That way, you won't have to fuss with special connector fittings.) The two-hole ears at top and bottom are adjustable and removable to suit differing wall thicknesses. This variety of box is also "gangable," which means you can join two boxes together by removing a side plate from each.

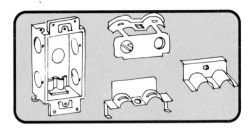

Internal clamps make for speedy hookups. The top one accommodates armored cable. the other two. nonmetallic sheathed cable.

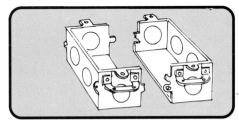

To "gang" boxes. remove one side from each and join the boxes with the screws that formerly held the sides in place.

Utility and Junction Boxes

All boxes must be made at least 1½ inches deep to comply with specifications in the Code. Most junction boxes—the ones in which you join wiring runs—are octagonal or square and are available only in the four-inch size. If you must mount a box on the surface of a wall, use the round-cornered variety called a utility or handy box.

Surface-mounted utility boxes come in 2- and 4-inch-wide sizes for one or two devices. Also use the square ones for junctions.

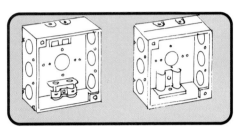

If the box won't be exposed. use one of these sharp-cornered types—for armored cable (left). or sheathed cable (right).

Ceiling Boxes

Ceiling boxes, used most often to hold fixtures, are usually round, octagonal, or square. (For junction work, use the roomier square ones.) Because of the weight of most fixtures, you'll have to anchor the box very solidly. So if you can't gain access to the ceiling joists, you'll have to mount the box in the plaster or drywall span between joists. (For more about this, see page 24.)

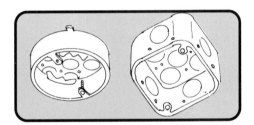

Ceiling boxes come with internal clamps and/or knockouts for separate connectors. Boxes nail to or are suspended between joists.

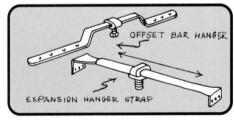

The straps on the bar hanger at top are recessed into the plaster and nailed to joist bottoms. Install the other from above.

Accessories

In addition to box connectors, many other accessories are available to solve about any wiring problem. For example, if you've installed thick planking over your old walls, your existing switch boxes are recessed too deeply to be safe. But a gadget called a *depth ring* can extend the box flush with the new surface. Check the sketches at right and electrical suppliers for more examples.

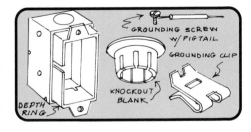

Accessories include a depth ring. grounding screw with pigtail. grounding clip. and a snap-in blank used to seal a knockout.

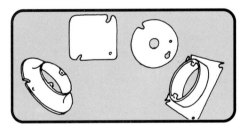

Every box must be covered in some way. Covers come in all sizes and shapes. ranging from metal disks to complex designs.

WHAT SIZE BOX SHOULD YOU USE?

Our concern here is simple: an overcrowded box increases the chances of short circuits.

The chart below shows the sizes and number of wires that you can safely fit inside boxes of various sizes. As you work with the numbers, keep these exceptions in mind: (1) Wires from a fixture on the box to wires in the box aren't counted. (2) A wire that enters and leaves the box without a splice counts as just one wire. (3) If the box contains a cable clamp, hickey, or fixture stud, reduce the number of permitted wires by one. (The reduction is only one, no matter how many items are in the box.) (4) Attached connectors aren't considered as devices in the box; count only those that are integral with the box. (5) Reduce one wire for each receptacle, switch, or other device in the box. (6) If a wire starts and ends in a box—such as a ground wire from the green terminal to the box—don't count it. (7) And when one or more bare grounding wires from nonmetallic sheathed cable run into a box, reduce by one the number of wires allowed.

Box Type	Size in Inches	Maximum Number of Wires				Box Type	Size in Inches	Maximum Number of Wires			
		No. 14	No. 12	No. 10	No. 8			No. 14	No. 12	No. 10	No. 8
Basic boxes	3x2x1 1/2	3	3	3	2	Ceiling and	4x1 1/2 round or	7	6	6	5
(for switches	3x2x2	5	4	4	3	junction	4x2 1/8 octagonal	10	9	8	7
and	3x2x2 1/4	5	4	4	3	boxes	4x1 1/2 square	10	9	8	7
receptacles)	3x2x2 1/2	6	5	5	4		4x2 1/8 square	15	13	12	10
	3x2x2 3/4	7	6	5	4		4 11/16x1 1/2 square	14	13	11	9
	3x2x3 1/2	9	8	7	6		4 11/16x2 1/8 square	21	18	16	14
Utility	4x2 1/8x1 1/2	5	4	4	3						
boxes	4x2 1/8x1 7/8	6	5	5	4						
	4x2 1/8x2 1/8	7	6	5	4						

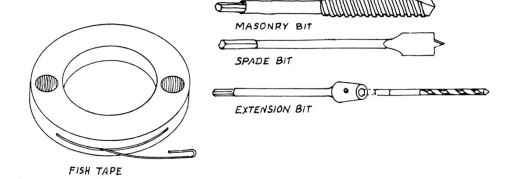

FISH TAPE

MASONRY BIT

SPADE BIT

EXTENSION BIT

TOOLS YOU'LL NEED FOR WIRING JOBS

On page 10 we talked about the tools you'll use to make general repairs. Now let's add a few more so you can work on those long runs between basement and attic.

Start out with a powerful *electric drill,* preferably one with a half-inch chuck. Arm yourself, too, with a good, sharp *spade bit* that can eat its way through 2x4s and their inevitable knots. Also buy an *extension bit* so you can make those deep cuts through double floor plates. And you'll need a carbide-tipped *masonry bit* to drill into masonry walls.

Round out your arsenal with a *conduit bender,* a *pipe cutter* (some pros still prefer a hacksaw), and the *fish tape* you bought for general repairs.

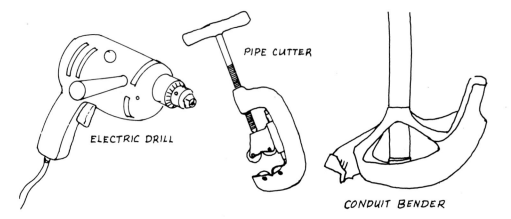

ELECTRIC DRILL

PIPE CUTTER

CONDUIT BENDER

EXTENDING EXISTING CIRCUITS

If you want to add just a couple of outlets or a new light fixture, you shouldn't have to go all the way to the service panel for your electricity. The two best places to borrow a little extra power are junction boxes and duplex receptacles.

If you have an unfinished basement, look there first. You should be able to find a junction box located as shown in the sketch below. If the circuit has excess capacity (see page 8) and your needs won't tax it, start your new line there. Or take your search to the attic, where you might find a box or two.

In the house proper, your best bet is a duplex receptacle like the one at right. Tie into one that has two unused terminals, providing the circuit has the power to spare.

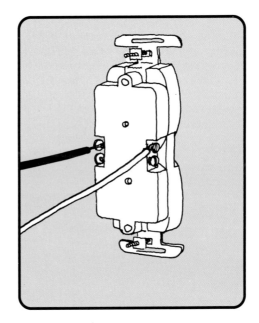

Note the four terminals on this duplex receptacle—two hot and two neutral. Extend the circuit by tying into the two unused ones.

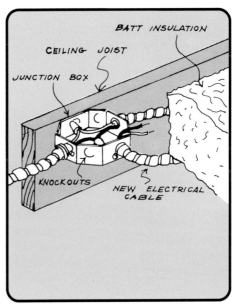

Extending a circuit from a junction box in the attic isn't difficult. Remove one of the knockouts and attach the cable.

Where Can You Tap In?

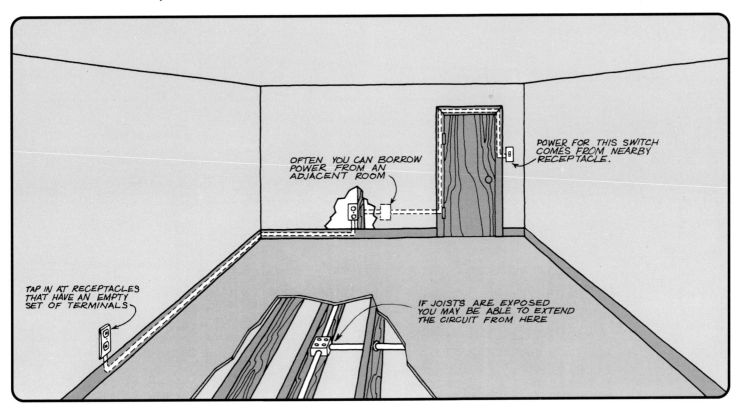

FISHING WIRES

Figuring out how to get your wiring from one spot to another—and then doing it—can be the biggest challenge of your electrical project. It takes time, patience, and a basic knowledge of construction techniques. But it also can be the most rewarding part of the job because once you've succeeded in pulling wires through an "impossible" maze of walls, ceilings, and floors, you know you've really accomplished something.

Expect to find a 2x4 plate in the bottom of each wall, double plates at the top, and possibly—heaven forbid—2x4 fire blocking crosswise between studs, halfway up the walls. If you have a chimney on an interior wall, try dangling a chain down alongside it; you may have found the best spot to run wire from the basement to the attic.

You'll have some patching jobs facing you when the wiring is complete, too. Again, consult a carpentry manual for advice about these jobs.

From Unfinished Spaces

  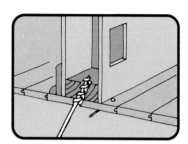

First, determine about where you want the outlet to be; then check to make certain you're not cutting into a stud.

Cut the opening in the wall, then carefully remove the baseboard and drill an angled locator hole in the floor.

Slip a 16d nail into the hole to mark the spot, then angle up through the plate from below with a brace and long bit.

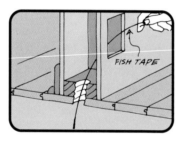  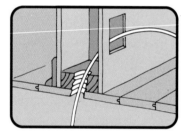

Thread fish tape up from below and have someone help guide the tip of it through the outlet hole and into the room.

Hook the end of the sheathed cable to the tape and wrap the junction with electrician's tape to ensure a smooth pull.

Pull the tape and the cable into the basement, then proceed to wire the outlet and mount it in the wall hole.

Through Finished Walls

 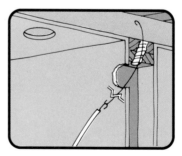 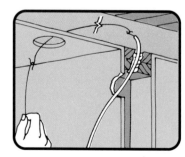

To get cable from a switch to a new ceiling fixture—without access from above—cut a hole in the wall near the ceiling.

Auger an angled hole up through the top plates, fasten the tape to the cable, then shove the other end of the tape into the cavity.

Fish a second tape into the ceiling, hook onto the first one, and pull the cable: fish the other end of the cable to the switch.

MOUNTING WALL BOXES

When you have access to exposed studs, you literally can mount a box a minute. But if you have to hunt for the studs, cut openings, and use special installation methods, plan on spending at least a half hour per box—and sometimes a lot longer if you run into complications such as a framing member you hadn't expected to encounter.

When placing the boxes, remember that switches usually go 48 to 50 inches above the floor; receptacles, 12 to 16 inches above the floor. Also keep in mind that the Code requires that receptacles be placed so that no point along any wall is more than six feet from an outlet. Note: always mount boxes so they'll be flush with the finished wall surface.

In finished spaces, your order of attack should be to locate and cut your openings, dry-fit the boxes, fish the cable, attach it to the box, then install the box permanently, as shown below. From that point on, it's a matter of patching walls, if necessary, and hooking up your new switches, receptacles, and fixtures.

In Unfinished Space

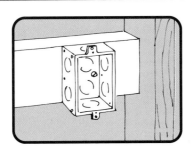

To mount a box away from a stud. just nail a 2x4 crosspiece between two studs and screw the box to the crosspiece.

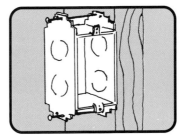

This box comes with two 16d nails. Simply hold it where you want it and whack the nails into the side of the stud.

Place this box in the desired position on the wall. Then nail through the bracket and into the stud. as illustrated.

In Paneling and Drywall

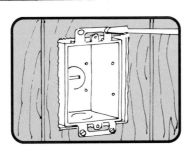

If the paneling is sturdy enough. just cut a hole. insert the box. and screw through the two ears into the paneling.

Shove this box into the drywall hole. then tighten the screws (these draw up holding clamps on ·each side of the box).

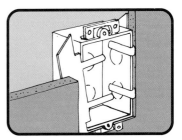

For a box without holding clamps, position box supports on each side of it (behind the drywall). and bend the flaps to anchor it.

In Lath and Plaster

Cut a small peek hole so you can center the box on a lath. Then draw around the box or use a template to mark the cut.

Cut away the plaster with a chisel. drill starter holes. then carefully cut the lath with a sharp keyhole or compass saw.

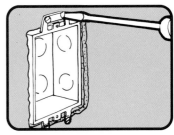

Enough lath should remain at top and bottom so you can screw the box directly to the lath strips through the ears.

MOUNTING CEILING BOXES FROM ABOVE

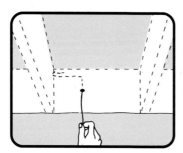

Drill a ¼-inch hole. slip an L-shaped piece of wire into it. and spin the wire to confirm an obstacle-free space above.

Widen the hole to an inch. Chuck a long extension and bit into your drill and bore a locator hole in the attic floor above.

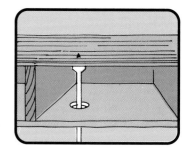

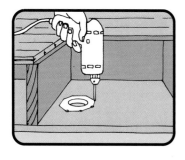

Cut out and save the flooring. draw an outline of the box, and drill starter holes all around the perimeter of the cutline.

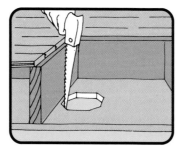

Cut the box opening with a keyhole saw. If you're working with plaster. deeply score it from below with a utility knife.

If you've spaced the hole the right distance from a joist. mount a box equipped with a bracket, as shown.

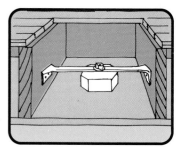

Otherwise. you'll need a box with its own adjustable bar hanger. Screw the ends of the hanger to neighboring joists.

MOUNTING CEILING BOXES FROM BELOW

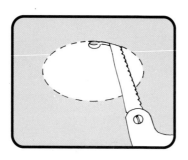
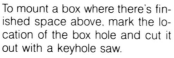

To mount a box where there's finished space above. mark the location of the box hole and cut it out with a keyhole saw.

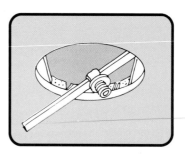

Insert a bar hanger and rest it on the ceiling. (Don't use this method to support anything heavier than a porcelain fixture.)

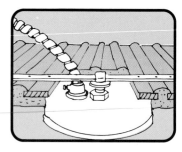

Remove the center knockout in a round ceiling box. slip the box onto the hanger stud. and screw on the anchoring nut.

To handle heavier fixtures. first cut a groove in the ceiling. extending it to the joist on either side of the intended position.

Cut a box hole in the center. and screw an offset bracket-and-box combination to the bottom of the joists: patch the grooves.

Here's a typical full-access installation for a recessed fixture. Note the use of headers to provide support.

WIRING RECEPTACLES AND SWITCHES

Compared to the hassles often involved in getting wires to a new receptacle or switch box, installing the devices themselves is a breeze. And after you've completed this final "finishing" phase comes the moment of truth when you restore power and find out if everything really works.

Learning how to hook up receptacles won't take long. You simply connect a black, hot wire to one of the brass terminals on each device, and a white, neutral to one of its silver-colored terminals. If the circuit will continue on from there, you then connect a second set of hot and neutral wires to the second set of terminals.

Switches, on the other hand, require a bit more thinking. First, you have to figure out where the switch is located relative to the source and the fixture it will control. Will power flow through the switch to the fixture, or vice versa?

Second, remember that a switch interrupts only the hot leg of the circuit. This means that if current will come to the fixture first, you must make a "switch loop" by connecting the *white* wire to the power source and switch, and the black to the switch and fixture. Since the white wire serves as a hot lead, it should be marked with black tape at each end.

If, however, current will come to the switch first and then to the fixture, you don't need to connect the neutral wires to the switch at all. You simply attach the black wires to each of the switch's terminals and "jump" the neutrals, as shown in the next-to-last drawing.

Note that in all the illustrations, we've left out grounding wires so the others will be easier to trace. To learn more about wiring switches and receptacles, see page 14; turn to page 39 for more about fixtures.

Receptacles

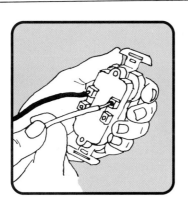 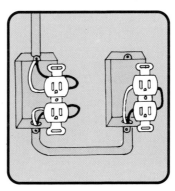 

In slot-type (sometimes called back-wired) receptacles. you just shove the hot wire into one slot. the neutral wire into the other.

To tie a second receptacle into the line. run wires from the empty set of terminals on the existing receptacle to the new one.

Fold the wires carefully into the box. then screw the receptacle to the box: align the plate before tightening the screws.

Two-Way Switches

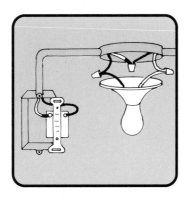 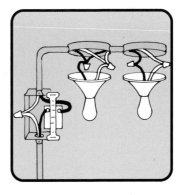 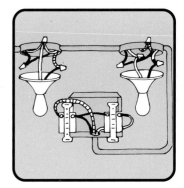

When you want the switch beyond a fixture (power comes from right). wire it like this. The white switch wire must be coded black.

When the switch is in the middle of the run. wire it this way to control two fixtures: power comes from the bottom.

When two switches in the same box control separate fixtures. use a three-wire cable, as shown. Power comes from the left.

Three- and Four-Way Switches

Three-way switches aren't what their name implies. They control lights from two locations, not three. Typically, you'll install one at the top of stairs, another at the bottom; both will operate the fixture lighting your stairway. But don't limit them to just this one use. Three-ways also are adaptable to many other lighting situations.

Though these switches are different from their simpler two-way cousins,

they're actually easy to understand if you learn these three bits of information: (1) A three-way switch has three terminals—a dark-colored one for the "common" wire, and two lighter-colored ones for the "traveler" wires. (2) Always attach the incoming hot wire (black) to the common terminal of one switch and always run a hot wire (black or a white wire marked black) from the common terminal of the second switch directly to the black wire on the fixture. (3) Always connect the two traveler terminals of one switch to the traveler terminals on the other switch.

You'll need to get four-way switches into the act whenever you want to control a light from more than two locations. Just remember to install a three-way switch nearest the power source, another nearest the light, and the four-way switches in between.

The wiring diagrams below will show you how to handle the most common installations. (We've left out the grounding wires to make the sketches easier to follow.)

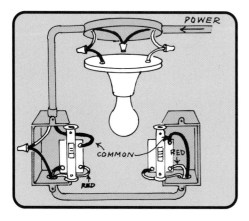

Here, the hot wire from the source passes through the fixture box and connects to the common terminal of the switch at left.

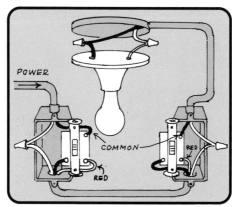

This is one of the fairly rare three-way installations in which the white neutral isn't pressed into service as a hot wire.

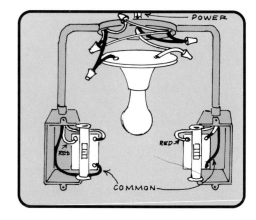

In this situation, the white wire serves as a traveler between switches. Indicate that it's "hot" with black tape or paint.

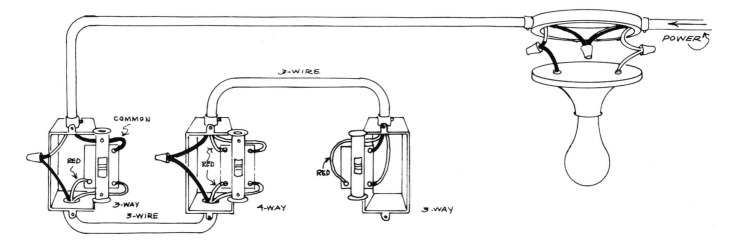

A four-way switch is wired between two three-way switches in this circuit so the light can be controlled from three locations. Note that two-wire cable (plus grounding wire) is all that's needed between the fixture and the first switch, but three-wire cable is required between switches. The neutrals take on added roles as travelers going from one switch to the next, and as the hot wire returning from the switches to the fixture. You can easily pick out the four-way switch: it has an extra terminal.

ADDING NEW CIRCUITS

Whenever you add on a room or take over unfinished space, you'll want to plan how you're going to run electricity to the new area. Chances are, you'll be doing two types of wiring jobs—burrowing behind and around finished surfaces, and breezing through the new construction.

The first step is necessary to get you from the service panel to the new space. From then on, you should be performing your craft after the rough framing is in, but before any finishing is done. (In a few rare cases, you won't have to go all the way to the service panel to start your circuits. Generally, though, an entire room will require more current than any nearby circuit can supply via the tapping strategies shown on page 21.)

Start at the service panel—but *don't* connect the wires to the box's terminals. Instead, fish all of your wiring (see page 22) through the walls, floors, and/or ceilings, as necessary. You'll probably be working with nonmetallic sheathed cable because you can't use rigid conduit without tearing out a lot of framing and finish materials. (Some local codes require the use of armored cable, so be sure to find out what's acceptable in your area.)

If your new room will require only a couple of circuits, you'll need to run only a single three-conductor cable from the panel; for a bigger multicircuit add-on, consider running heavier cable from the main service panel to a new subpanel in the new space, then splitting off the new circuits from the subpanel.

When you get to the area of new construction, use a spade bit to drill wiring holes through the centers of the studs and joists. This minimizes the chances of a nail being driven into the wire later. If you're forced to drill a hole closer than 1½ inches from the front of the wood, cover the spot with a piece of metal plate at least 1/16 inch thick.

After the wiring is in, mount the boxes where needed (see pages 23 and 24). This stage of the project also will take place in the new area and should go quickly because you simply nail the boxes to the sides of the exposed framing. Then install the switches, receptacles, and fixtures (see pages 25–26, and 36–42).

Connecting to the Service Panel

This is the part of the job you may or may not want to do yourself. Some experts recommend hiring a licensed electrician to do all work inside the service panel (or box) itself; others say that if you take precautions and pay attention to what you're doing, you shouldn't have any trouble.

If you choose to make your own connections at the panel, the first thing you want to do is to remove or open the front cover and flip off the main breaker or pull the main fuses. (Caution: this shuts off all the branch circuits in your home, but those big wires coming into the box up top will still be live. Stay away from them!) Strip the wires you'll be bringing into the box, making sure they're long enough to curl around inside the box and reach the proper terminals. Then remove a knockout from the side of the box and anchor the cable or conduit to the box with a cable clamp or conduit connector.

For a fuse box, connect the black wire to the terminal screw on the fuse holder, and screw the white wire to the bus bar to which all of the other white wires are connected. Attach the ground wire to the ground strip, which in some cases may be the same terminal used for the white wires. Screw in a fuse of the amperage you need, replace the inner cover of the box, and reinstall the main fuses to test the circuit.

For a circuit breaker box, attach the white neutral wire and bare grounding wire to the neutral bar. Fasten the black wire to a new circuit breaker, and install it. Flip the main breaker on and test the circuit. (Before you put the panel cover on again you'll need to remove the proper knockout[s] to accommodate the new breaker[s].)

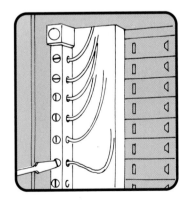

On many bus bars, you slip the end of the wire into a slot, then drive a screw tightly against the wire. Tug to be sure it's secure.

Installing this type of breaker is a one-handed job: simply push the breaker contacts into the appropriate slots.

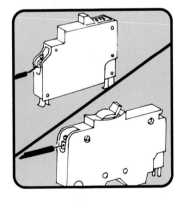

The breaker shown at left is held in position by its friction ears: the style at right snaps in place after you've connected a hot wire to it.

When working with the innards of a service panel, you're safest if you stand on a board and keep one hand in your pocket.

HEAVY-DUTY CIRCUITS

Appliances that need heavy-duty circuits (120/240 volts or 240 volts only) must be wired according to strict guidelines, so find out what's required in your locality. You'll usually be working with special heavy-duty receptacles and plugs—even for built-in appliances that you'd normally expect to wire directly to a junction box. That's because the Code requires that you be able to disconnect a built-in unit in case of electrical emergencies. In some situations, this means a separate switch wired from the service panel, but usually the disconnect device is simply a heavy-duty receptacle into which a matching cord-connected plug is inserted.

Receptacles and plugs are commonly identified as 2-pole 2-wire, 2-pole 3-wire, 3-pole 3-wire, 3-pole 4-wire, and so forth. The number of poles indicates the number of wires that normally carry current. If there is one more wire than poles, this means the receptacle or plug has an extra connection for a separate grounding wire. Never connect a current-carrying wire to this terminal.

240-Volt Plugs and Receptacles

Hook together two 120-volt circuits and you have a 240-volt circuit. These consist of just two hot wires (plus an equipment ground); you don't need a neutral. This means that if you use ordinary two-wire cable (it will have a black and a white wire), you should mark the ends of the white wire with black paint or tape to indicate that the white wire also is hot.

Manufacturers of receptacles and plugs design their products so a plug of a certain voltage and wiring scheme generally will fit only a receptacle with identical characteristics, and will not mesh with a receptacle carrying a lower or higher amperage/voltage rating.

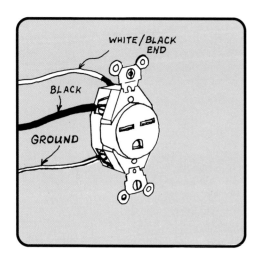

In this 240-volt, two-wire-plus-ground receptacle, the top two terminals are for the current-carrying wires.

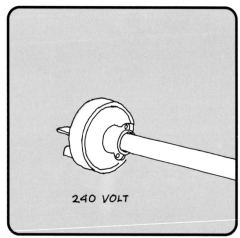

This 240-volt plug is a mate for the receptacle at left, and is wired identically. A protective sleeve covers the wiring.

120/240-Volt Plugs and Receptacles

Sometimes, an appliance such as a range must be fed with a 120/240-volt supply. That's because the burners may need 240 volts at the higher settings but only 120 for lower heats. (The timers, lights, and so forth also run off 120.) So a special three- or four-prong plug and receptacle is made for this installation. (Three wires carry current; the fourth is for grounding.)

Heavy-duty components come in dozens of configurations—each for specific voltage and amperage requirements. (The chart opposite illustrates a few of the types.) Some plugs are designed so they can't be inserted or removed without twisting.

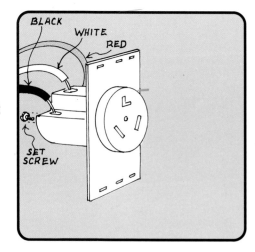

This 120/240-volt receptacle has three current-carrying wires—a white neutral (for the 120-volt portion) and a red and black.

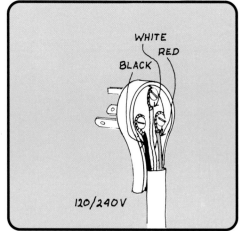

When you get to the plug, simply match up its terminals with the receptacle terminals, then wire by color accordingly.

INSTALLING MAJOR APPLIANCES

If you're running wiring for a new appliance, carefully read the articles of the Code pertaining to appliance circuits. Several decisions face you, the main ones being which size of wire and circuit breaker (or fuse) to use, and what types of plugs and receptacles are right for the job.

The chart below summarizes what your research will probably reveal—but be sure to check any appliance's rating before you size the circuit. (If it's given in watts, remember that you can simply divide by the voltage to get an amperage figure.)

Note, too, that 240-volt plugs and receptacles aren't as standardized as 120-volt devices. Not only do their configurations vary according to the amperages they're designed to handle, but sometimes even a receptacle and plug rated at the same amperage won't mate. The chart shows only some of the dozens of possibilities.

Will you need a special heavy-duty plug and receptacle at all? Again, the answer depends on what the Code says about the appliance in question. It talks about three types of appliances—portable, stationary, and fixed—and spells out different rules for each. A portable appliance, such as a microwave oven, is one that's quite mobile. The stationary variety (a slide-in range, dryer, etc.) can be moved fairly readily but is rarely shifted from its original point of installation. Fixed appliances (water heaters, cooktops, wall ovens, etc.) are permanently installed.

SIZING HEAVY-DUTY CIRCUITS			
Appliance	Electrical Requirements	Wire Size	Plug/Receptacle
Electric dryer	120/240 volts, up to 30 amps	#10	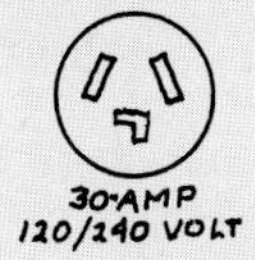 30-AMP 120/240 VOLT
Electric water heater	240 volts, 20 to 30 amps	#12 for 20 amps or less #10 for 30 amps or less	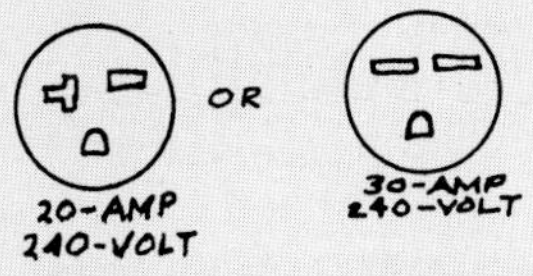 20-AMP 240-VOLT OR 30-AMP 240-VOLT
Range	Combination oven/cooktop units typically draw up to 50 amps at 120/240 volts. Check local code to determine if you need a plug and receptacle, or should wire directly to a junction box.	Most require two #6 hot wires and a #8 neutral; for small units, you may be able to use two #8 hot wires and a #10 neutral.	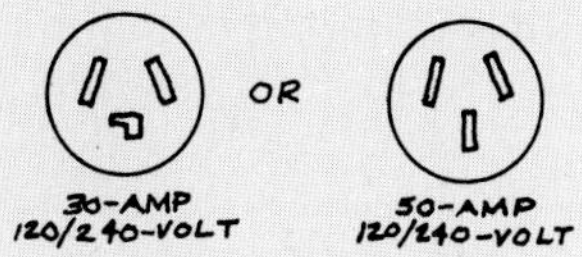 30-AMP 120/240-VOLT OR 50-AMP 120/240-VOLT
Separate oven and cooktop	Connect both to a single, 50-amp, 120/240-volt circuit, or provide separate 30-amp circuits for each.	For a single-circuit installation, see *Range* above; 30-amp circuits require #10 wire.	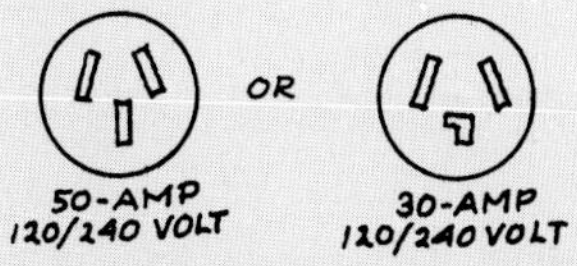 50-AMP 120/240 VOLT OR 30-AMP 120/240 VOLT
Microwave oven, refrigerator, dishwasher, clothes washer, gas dryer	These units typically draw less than 15 or 20 amps and require only a 120-volt circuit. Each should have a separate circuit, though.	#12	 15-AMP 120-VOLT
Air conditioner	Window units vary according to their BTU capacity—from less than 15 amps at 120 volts up to 30 amps at 240 volts.	#12 for 20 amps or less #10 for 30 amps or less	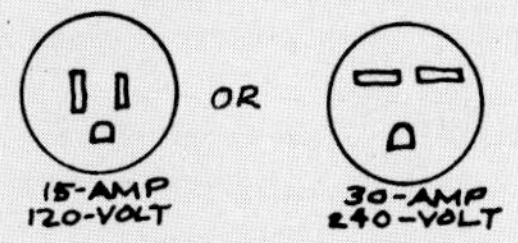 15-AMP 120-VOLT OR 30-AMP 240-VOLT

GROUNDING APPLIANCES

Big electricity users should be grounded to provide added insurance against injury from shock if a circuit's fuse or breaker should fail to react when needed. If your home's receptacles are properly grounded (see page 9), the third wire of the appliance's power cord will ground the unit. Otherwise, or if local codes require it, you should ground your appliances as shown here.

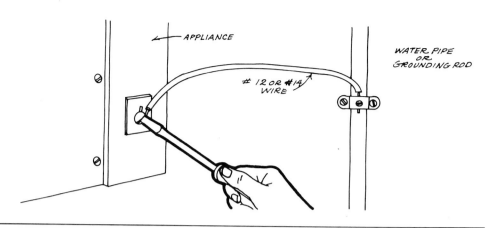

TROUBLESHOOTING APPLIANCES

When an appliance or power tool conks out—or begins to malfunction—you may need professional help to get it running smoothly again. But before you call for service, see if you can systematically isolate what's wrong using this process of elimination.

Start with the most obvious possibilities. Is the machine plugged in? Are its controls properly set? Next, go to the service panel and look for a tripped breaker or blown fuse. If you find one, reset the breaker (or replace the fuse).

If the circuit goes off again, you can be fairly sure that either there's a short within the unit or its cord, or that the entire circuit is overloaded. Sometimes, just unplugging an appliance and

peering into its innards will reveal a bare wire that has grounded out.

If, on the other hand, you *don't* find a breaker or fuse out, you know that the circuit is live. Double-check this by testing the unit's receptacle.

The drawings below illustrate where to look for problems. The owner's manual for your appliance may have additional suggestions.

If jiggling the plug gets an appliance going again. either the plug or—more rarely—the receptacle is faulty.

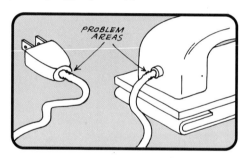

If a cord goes bad, it usually occurs where it attaches to the appliance or near the plug. See pages 12 and 13 on replacing cords and plugs.

Sometimes wiggling a switch gets results. If so. the switch should be replaced—a job you may not be able to do yourself.

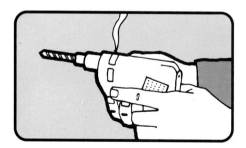

Motors that spark. smoke. or smell usually need new brushes. Don't use the device until it's been repaired.

With larger appliances. you may be able to track down the source of a malfunction with some careful listening.

WORKING WITH LOW-VOLTAGE WIRING

Doorbells, chimes, intercoms, thermostats, and even some lighting systems run on low voltages that are "stepped down" by a special transformer from 120-volt household current to levels ranging between six and 30 volts. These electrical subsystems can be installed without boxes, circuit breakers, fuses, or special grounding procedures.

Working with low-voltage circuits is ideal work for do-it-yourselfers, not only because the current is so limited that you can't cause fires, but also because the voltage is low enough that any shocks you get are at most a tickle.

If you're replacing old wiring, you'll probably be installing what's often called bell wire—a No. 18 gauge wire with a thin coating of plastic insulation. You splice it simply by twisting together two ends and covering them with tape. Be sure to buy different colors of wire so you'll know at a glance which is which

when you're ready to make the final connections. And before you buy wire, find out whether you're working on a two-wire or three-wire system.

Of course, if you're installing a low-voltage device in a home where none exists, your first step will be to run a circuit from the service panel to a conveniently located junction box. Then add a transformer and go from there.

Doorbells and Chimes

The most popular use for low-voltage wiring is the common doorbell—or, in some installations, chimes. The low-voltage part of the system starts at the transformer, which is usually in the 6- to 8-volt range for doorbells, or 15 to 20 volts for chimes. A few models are even multi-voltaged, giving you the option of

choosing the terminal—and voltage—you need. Transformers vary, so if you're replacing a bad one, be sure to get a unit that will be compatible with your existing system.

In old installations, you may find the transformer mounted near the junction box or even on the box cover. But in newer homes, it's usually fastened to the side of the service panel.

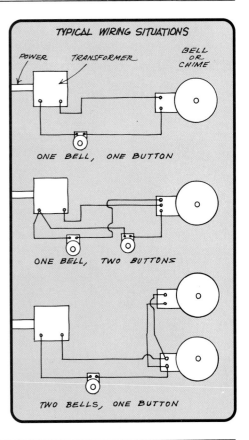

TYPICAL WIRING SITUATIONS

ONE BELL, ONE BUTTON

ONE BELL, TWO BUTTONS

TWO BELLS, ONE BUTTON

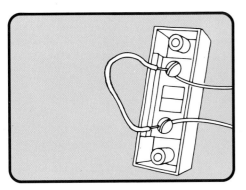

To check out a doorbell button, use a jumper wire, or a screwdriver as discussed in the copy below. If bell rings, button is shot.

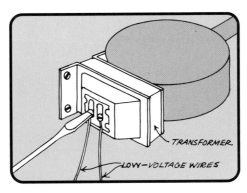

A threaded fitting on this transformer extends through a knockout in the junction box and is held by a retaining nut.

Troubleshooting Procedures

Running down a problem in your doorbell (or chime) system is mainly a process of elimination. If the bell works sporadically, check out the button first. Unscrew it from the wall and hold a screwdriver across the two contact points. If the bell doesn't ring, clean the contact points with emery cloth and

make sure the contacts touch when the button is pushed.

Assuming the button works, check the bell and transformer for loose connections. If they're tight, hold a screwdriver across the transformer's bell-wire connections. If you don't get a weak spark, replace the transformer. If you do see even the faintest spark, the transformer is fine, and your search narrows down to the

bell itself or to the wiring. The easiest way to check the bell is to disconnect it, clean it thoroughly, rub the contacts with emery cloth, then hook it up directly to the *bell-wire* connections at the transformer. If you don't get a ring, the bell is shot; if you do, you'd better start replacing the wire—a tedious, last-resort measure.

OUTDOOR WIRING

Whether it's an outdoor receptacle installation you've been considering, or a more extensive project such as running a branch circuit to a new shed or backyard light, the principles you learned for your interior work still apply outdoors. Only the equipment changes —and that only slightly.

Outdoor wiring does involve a few added precautions, though. For example, whenever undertaking any outdoor wiring project, use either metal conduit with Type-TW wires pulled through it, or UF cable, a tough, highly moisture-resistant sheathed cable. Some local codes specify one in particular, so check with code authorities on this. While you're there, also ask if there are any local restrictions concerning who does the work and how it's to be done.

If you use cable, you're still required to protect it with conduit whenever above ground. Keep in mind, too, that cable should be buried at least 12 inches below the surface. Rigid conduit needs to go only six inches underground; thinner conduit needs 12 inches of earth protection.

To guard against serious shock, always protect all outside circuits containing receptacles with a ground-fault circuit interrupter or GFCI (see page 35).

The outdoor components shown below, though they look similar to ones used inside, have watertight features such as gasket seals, spring-loaded covers, and rubber-sealed connections.

WEATHERPROOF COMPONENTS

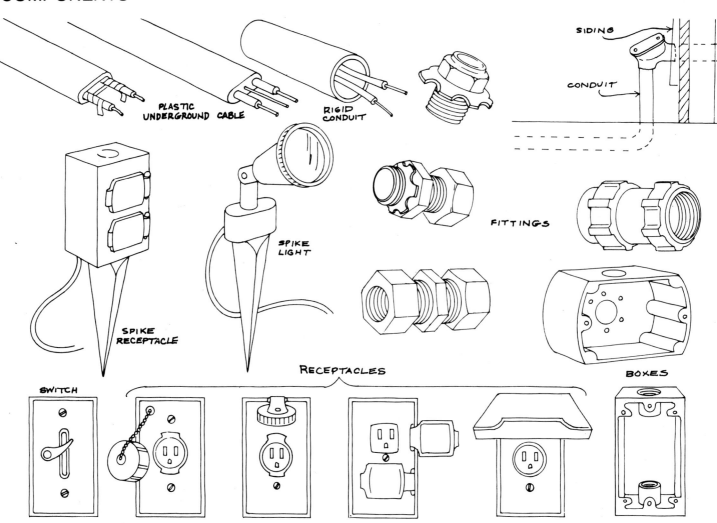

PLASTIC UNDERGROUND CABLE

RIGID CONDUIT

SIDING

CONDUIT

SPIKE RECEPTACLE

SPIKE LIGHT

FITTINGS

RECEPTACLES

BOXES

SWITCH

GETTING WIRES THROUGH A WALL

Cutting a hole in an exterior wall isn't something you'll want to do without some planning. Where you make the incision should depend on your success in finding a circuit that's underused, how far you have to go to tie into a feeder line, and where you want to locate your new light or receptacle.

In some locations, you can run sheathed cable through the wall to the exterior box; in other places, you're required to use conduit or armored cable. Find out what codes permit.

In most cases it's best to install a junction box back to back with the new exterior box, then connect the two with conduit or armored cable.

Another way to get power for an outdoor add-on is to tap off of an existing exterior fixture. Special fittings and adapters make it easy for you to tie into the old fixture box. But before deciding on this approach, make sure that the present circuit has the extra capacity you need (see page 8).

INSTALLING AN EXTERIOR RECEPTACLE

The easiest outdoor electrical job of all is installing a receptacle. This amounts to little more than locating and cutting the hole, then mounting a weatherproof box on the surface or recessing it into the wall (this is the best way to go,

even though it requires more work). Remember that a ground-fault interrupter must be installed in any outdoor circuit to guard against a potentially dangerous shock if anything should go wrong.

One of the most overlooked—but obvious—locations for an exterior receptacle is the wall facing a deck or patio.

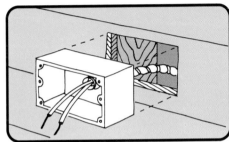

Carefully size the opening so the special waterproof box will fit snugly and minimize heat-robbing gaps.

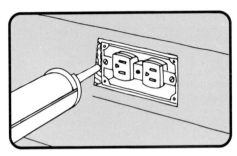

Install the receptacle (see page 35 for a ground-fault-protected type), and caulk as shown before screwing on the faceplate.

INSTALLING AN EXTERIOR LIGHT

These days, security isn't far from anyone's mind. That's why it's comforting to know that a flick of a switch can turn a dark, shadowy backyard into one flooded with light. If you can't perform this kind of magic,

you'd be smart to install a security light or two. (See pages 34, 43, and 44 for tips on where to put them to give you the most safety and security.) One of the easiest locations to work with is under an overhang.

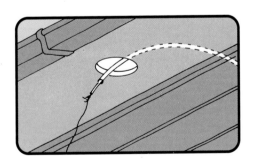

Make an opening for a switch box in the room below. then fish a sheathed or armored cable to it through a hole in the soffit.

Fasten the cable to an outdoor fixture box with the appropriate box connector. screw the box to the soffit. and wire the fixture.

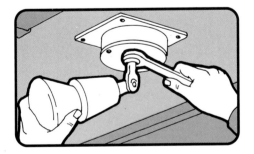

After connecting the cable wires to the fixture wires with wire nuts. mount the special outdoor fixture to the box.

RUNNING WIRES UNDERGROUND

You'll quite literally "dig" running underground wiring, so plan on spending some time in the trenches. If you're planning a lengthy run, consider renting a trencher for a few hours. Though expensive, this tool makes quick work of this otherwise laborious task.

(See page 32 for depth requirements for cable and conduit.)

Start your wiring project by planning your routes, including where you want to go through the wall. Then run power to a new junction box nearby, and drill through the wall. It's best to use a short piece of rigid conduit to make the through-the-wall connection between the box and an exterior connector called an LB fitting. This fitting enables you to make the sharp 90-degree turn downward and also has a removable plate that takes the strain out of pulling wires.

Remember that you have to run conduit from the fitting to the bottom of your trench—and at the other end between the trench and the receptacle or lamppost.

Carefully remove and save the sod before you dig the trench; pile the loose dirt on a tarp or piece of plastic sheeting.

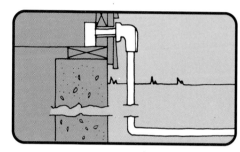

Though the LB fitting at the wall opening has a removable plate, there's not enough room inside to make connections.

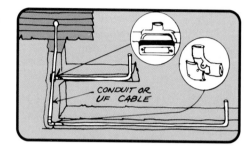

If you use rigid conduit throughout, you can buy special fittings called *bodies* to make the T-junctions and turns you need.

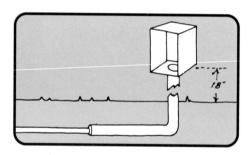

A receptacle should be at least 18 inches from the ground, and its wiring must be protected above grade by conduit.

Stabilize all receptacles below ground with concrete; use either a big coffee can or a concrete block as your form.

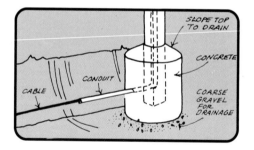

For lamps, run the conduit or cable up the center of the post, then set the post in a concrete pier with a sloped top.

INSTALLING AUTOMATIC LIGHTING CONTROLS

One way to be sure your security light is on every night is to wire it directly to an automatic control. You'll find two types available—photocells and timers. Both usually come with easy-to-follow installation instructions. Photocells, of course, need to be outdoors, but timers should be installed inside.

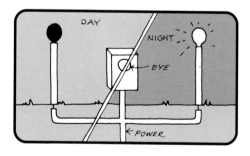

Photocells turn lights on at dusk, off at dawn. Include a switch as well, so you can manually override the photocell.

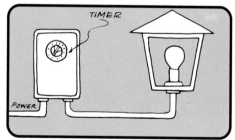

Timers let you choose when the lights should go on and off. One model can take the place of a standard light switch.

INSTALLING GROUND-FAULT INTERRUPTERS

If one of your electrical tools or appliances goes haywire and starts leaking current, the grounding wire will carry off most of the errant electricity. But the key word here is *most*, because there may be enough other current zapping around to make you an instant conductor anyway. As little as 200 milliamperes—about enough to light a 25-watt bulb—can kill you if you happen to be touching plumbing components or standing on wet earth. That's why the Code requires that all new 15- and 20-amp outdoor receptacles and all new bathroom circuits be protected by a ground-fault circuit interrupter.

A GFCI is an amazing device in that it trips the circuit whenever even a tiny leakage occurs. And the shutoff action is so fast, there's not enough time for you to be injured. Shown at right are three commonly available types of GFCIs.

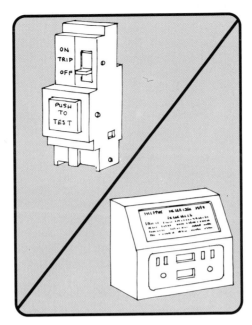

Install the GFCI at left in your service panel. Plug the other model into a receptacle, then plug an appliance or tool into it.

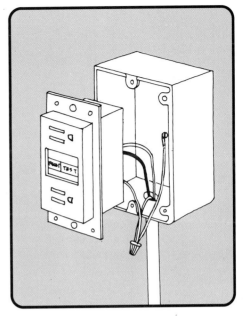

This GFCI replaces a standard receptacle and is a natural for outdoor use—mounted on a wall or on conduit in your yard.

USING ELECTRICITY WISELY

Ever wondered exactly how much it costs to burn a light or run an appliance? To find out, all you need to do is multiply the wattage the device consumes by the numbers (or fractions) of hours you use it. Divide this result by 1,000 and multiply it by the price you pay per kilowatt-hour for electricity. Your electric utility can provide price information.

If you can't find a wattage figure on an appliance's rating plate, simply multiply its amperage by its voltage.

The table at right compares operating costs for major appliances and tells how you can reduce the amounts of energy they use. For more about lighting, turn to the following page.

HOW THRIFTY ARE YOUR APPLIANCE HABITS?		
Appliance	**Relative Operating Cost**	**How You Can Save**
Refrigerator, Freezer	The biggest energy eaters in any kitchen. Auto-defrost models use as much as 50 percent more than manual-defrost types.	If you can do without the convenience, buy a manual-defrost; if not, energy-saving automatic types are worth the extra money you'll have to pay for them.
Range	Usually the number-two consumer, depending on your family's cooking and baking needs. Self- and continuous-cleaning ovens are more costly.	Cook small meals in pressure cookers, microwaves, or other small appliances. A meat thermometer used in conjunction with a timer minimizes wasteful oven-peeking.
Dishwasher	Third or fourth. Most of the energy goes for heating water, so run only full loads and select short cycles.	Eliminating the drying cycle can cut operating costs by at least one-third.
Washer, Dryer	Third or fourth. Again, the less water a machine uses, the less it costs to operate. On dryers, auto-dry settings can save electricity, but actually not too much.	Run cold-water loads whenever possible and use the lowest water level necessary. Longer spin periods cut down drying times.

LIGHTING

Vision specialists maintain that almost 90 percent of what we know and feel comes to us via our eyes—making lighting the most informative of your home's systems. In too many households, though, it's also one of the most neglected.

Few of us live totally in the dark, of course. But because our eyes tend to compensate for light levels that are a bit too dim or too bright, it's easy to ignore a lighting problem that causes eyestrain, fatigue, or even accidents.

Inefficient lighting wastes energy, too. Without enough illumination in a particular area, you may be turning on every lamp or fixture in the general vicinity—or overcompensating with high-wattage bulbs.

How much lighting is enough? And what can you do to achieve the proper level? This section begins by answering the first question, then goes on to explain the many different ways you can approach the second.

Good lighting starts with the right bulb. For most of the lamps and fixtures in your home, you probably prefer the warm color quality and high adaptability of *incandescent* bulbs. In these, electricity charges a metal filament, causing it to glow as white heat. The higher the filament's electrical resistance, the more watts it consumes and the more light it gives.

Note, though, that wattage figures don't truly denote the amount of light a bulb puts out. This is expressed in *lumens,* and not all bulbs are equally efficient on a lumens-per-watt basis. If you're interested in comparing bulbs in this way, you'll find a lumen output rating on the bulb's paper sleeve, though not on the bulb itself.

As a class, incandescent bulbs are the least efficient—much of the energy they use is wasted producing heat, which eventually burns up the filament. Long-life bulbs give off less heat—and correspondingly less light—for the same amount of electricity.

Fluorescent and high intensity discharge (HID) lighting, though each has its own drawbacks, use far less electricity per lumen output than incandescent bulbs, and can last 10 to 30 times longer. More about these money and energy savers on pages 41–43.

General lighting visually expands a room's size and provides basic brightness. It usually consists of a ceiling or wall fixture. supplemented · with convenient portable lighting.

For living and sleeping areas. lighting experts recommend that you allow one watt per square foot with flush or pendant fixtures (see the opposite page). and 1.5 watts per square foot for recessed lights.

Kitchens. baths. and laundries need more illumination—as much as four watts per square foot for incandescent bulbs. and 1.5 watts for fluorescent tubes.

Task lighting lets you get a good look at what you're doing by focusing on countertops, sinks, workbenches, and your favorite reading spots.

Most tasks require 150 watts of incandescent or 40 watts of fluorescent lighting. For prolonged reading, though, you need 200 to 300 watts of incandescent, 60 to 80 fluorescent.

For countertops and workbenches, provide 120 watts of incandescent or 20 watts of fluorescent lighting for each three running feet of work surface. Fixtures should be mounted 14 to 22 inches above the surface.

Accent lighting provides architectural flavor. and sometimes does the job of general lighting as well. Use it to wash a wall. play up interesting textures. spotlight a fireplace. or dramatize a dining table.

With accent lighting. let your imagination be your guide as to how much is enough. Do try. though. to give rooms a variety of different accent lights. separately switched. so you can vary moods and suit different requirements. A wide spectrum of bulbs— incandescent. fluorescent. and HID—adds even more possibilities.

SELECTING FIXTURES

The most difficult thing about selecting light fixtures today is narrowing down the huge selection available. There's a fixture for every need, and for every budget. In fact, the possibilities are almost limitless once you realize that many lamp shops and hardware stores stock lamp components you can put together yourself.

The chart below discusses the various types of fixtures and some of their many uses. If after digesting this information, you're still not quite sure which type of fixture is right for you, go to a lighting store and talk with personnel there about your requirements. They should be able to guide you toward the most appropriate products.

YOUR LIGHTING FIXTURE OPTIONS

Type	Use
Surface	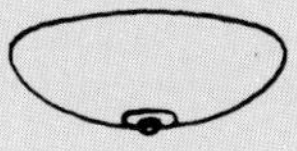 This old standby mounts directly on the ceiling's surface, distributing very even, shadowless general lighting. These must be shielded with translucent material to minimize glare, and should have sockets for several smaller bulbs rather than one or two big ones. A variation, the surface-mounted downlight, looks like a can or cylinder and provides task or accent lighting.
Dropped (suspended)	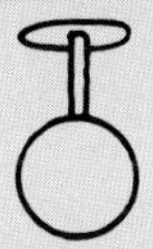 Pendants, chandeliers, and other dropped styles have many of the same characteristics as flush-mounted fixtures, and you can easily substitute one for the other. Because these are closer to eye level, glare can be a problem. Try using low-wattage bulbs or dimmer switches (see page 39). Hang fixtures 12 to 20 inches below an 8-foot ceiling or 30 to 36 inches above table height.
Recessed	 Recessed fixtures include fixed and aimable downlights, incandescent or fluorescent bulbs shielded by plastic diffusers, and even totally luminous ceilings. You can get a wide range of highlights and shadows with recessed lighting, but it requires more wattage—up to twice as much as other types.
Wall bracket	 Wall-mounted fixtures conserve space in tight quarters, serving as either task or accent lighting. For reading, mount them 15 to 20 inches to the left or right of the page, 48 inches above the floor.
Track	 Track lighting offers great versatility. You can add, subtract, or rearrange fixtures at will, aiming them in any direction you please. You get a very broad choice of modular fixtures, too—ranging from simple spot and floodlight bulb holders to framing projectors with special shutters to exactly control the spread of light. To learn about installing track lights, see page 40.
Cornice	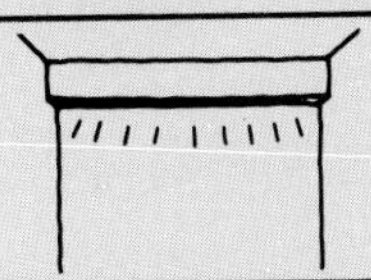 Cornices mount at the intersection of a wall and ceiling, bathing the wall with soft, downward light to dramatize draperies or other wall treatments. You can build a cornice treatment with 1x2 and 1x6 lumber. Mount the tube so its center is 6 inches from the wall. 
Valance	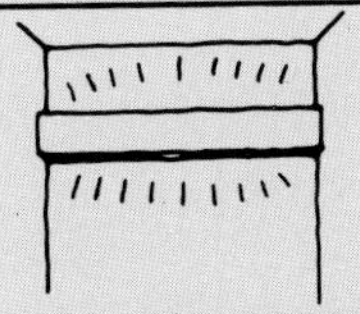 Valances resemble cornices, but they're installed lower on the wall often over draperies, providing both up- and downlight. To build one, you'll need 1x2- and 1x6-inch material and angle brackets, as shown at right. Top off the unit with a strip of plastic and you can also use it as a display shelf. 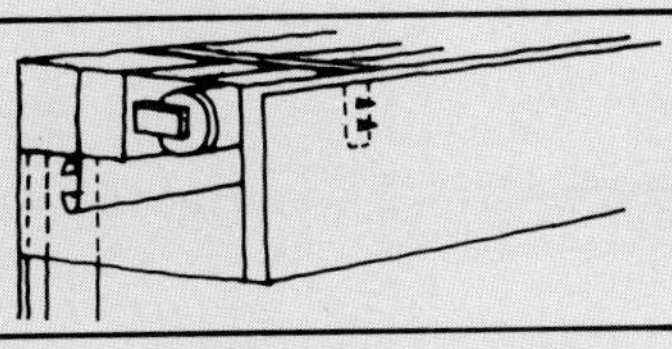
Cove	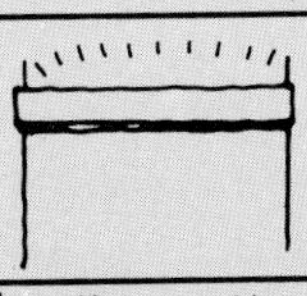 Cove lighting dramatizes a ceiling. You can buy commercial metal or plastic fixtures, or make your own with wood and angle brackets, as illustrated. Mount the light about a foot below ceiling level, and paint the inside white to maximize reflection. 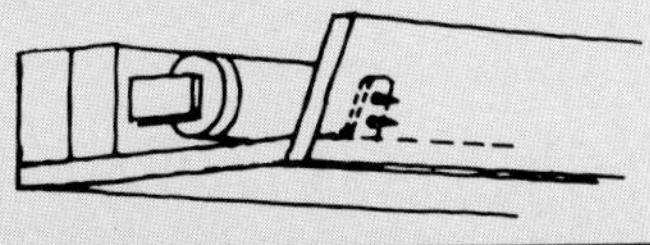
Under-cabinet	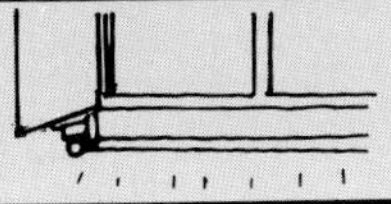 The simplest way to shed light on countertops is to attach fluorescent tubes to the undersides of cabinets, as shown. Shield them with skirting. Use the longest tubes that will fit, and fill at least two-thirds of the counter's total length.

INCAN-DESCENT LIGHTING

Incandescent fixtures operate much like the ordinary table lamp shown on page 12. A pair of *leads* serves as the cord, connecting the fixture's socket or *bulb holder* to house wiring. (For safety, these connections must always be made in a ceiling or wall box.)

But because fixtures don't permit as much air circulation, they get much hotter than table lamps. That's why bulb holders are usually made of nonmelting material, such as porcelain, and wired with high-temperature conductors.

It's also why you should never exceed the wattage specified on the unit's *canopy plate*—heat could melt the wires' insulation, causing a short circuit, a fire, or both.

Support systems vary (see below), but all of them secure the fixture to its electrical box—usually a four-inch octagon—and in some cases to the ceiling as well. Never support a fixture only with its leads.

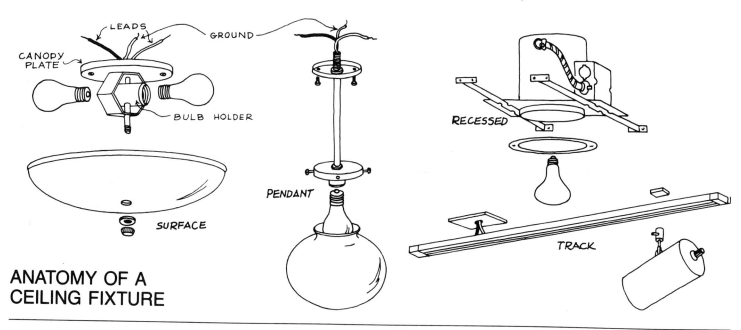

ANATOMY OF A CEILING FIXTURE

TROUBLESHOOTING FIXTURES

With a roll of electrical tape, a screwdriver, a pair of pliers, and a neon test light, you can track and solve most fixture problems. To eliminate any possibility of electrical shock, shut off power to the light, then double-check with your tester before touching the fixture. You may have to turn on the power later to make some of the tests called for below.

THINGS TO CHECK		
Symptom	**Causes**	**Cures**
No light	A burned-out light bulb. A broken or loose wire in the ceiling box. Switches occasionally go bad, too.	Replace bulb. Drop the fixture as shown on the opposite page, then check and tighten all connections. Check out the switch with a neon tester (see page 11); to learn about replacing switches, see page 14.
Fixture blows fuses	Frayed wires in the ceiling box may be shorting out, or a bulb socket may be defective.	Drop the fixture and examine the wires carefully; tape any bad spots. Test the socket (see page 11). Some sockets can be easily replaced; with others, you'll have to get a new fixture.
Light flickers	Suspect melted insulation or a failing socket. A dimmer may be going bad.	Tape or replace any wires that look dubious. Next, test the socket. If you still have a problem, you may have to replace the dimmer.

REPLACING A FIXTURE

Substituting a new fixture for an old one usually takes only a few minutes, if you have the right hardware. First shut off power at the service panel. Wall switches interrupt only the fixture's "hot" wire, so you still could get a shock through the neutral if the circuit is live.

Next, examine how the old fixture is attached. Some secure with bolts to a *strap,* as shown in the first drawing below; others mount with a *hickey* to a *stud* in the center of the box (third drawing); still others use a combination of these systems.

After that, just follow the sequence illustrated. Take care not to undo any other connections you may find in the box, and handle fixtures gently—most are made of lightweight metal that can be bent easily.

To learn about getting power to a location that had none before, see pages 15–27.

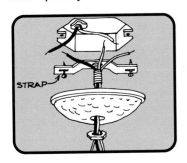

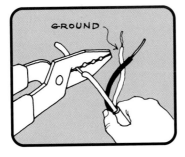

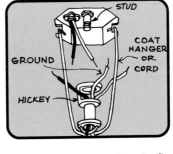

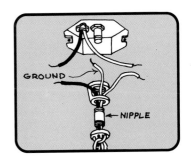

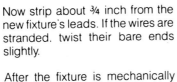

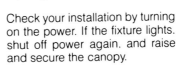

As you dismantle the old fixture. note how everything fits together. Strap mounting works best with lighter units.

Now strip about ¾ inch from the new fixture's leads. If the wires are stranded. twist their bare ends slightly.

Temporarily support a heavier fixture with a coat hanger or strong cord. as shown. Preassemble everything first.

Make sure all of the wires exit via the hickey's side, screw a nipple into it. then thread the hickey onto the stud.

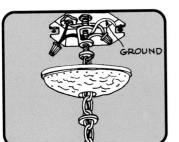

After the fixture is mechanically secure. make the electrical connections. then carefully coil up wires within the box.

Check your installation by turning on the power. If the fixture lights. shut off power again. and raise and secure the canopy.

INSTALLING A DIMMER SWITCH

Dimmers let you select lighting levels according to your needs and moods. And by reducing a bulb's wattage, they conserve some electrical energy and greatly prolong the bulb's life.

Install one as you would any switch (see page 14); don't overload the dimmer beyond the wattage limits specified on its housing. In three-way installations, make sure to use a dimmer designed for this use. Otherwise, you could burn out the unit.

And note that incandescent dimmers should be used only in incandescent lighting circuits, not to control motors or fluorescents.

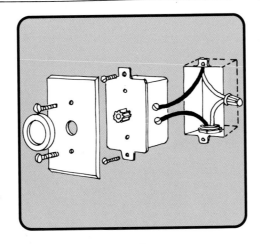

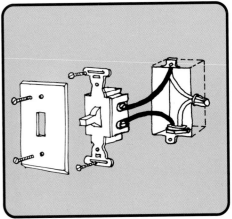

Hook up a rotary-type dimmer as shown. Tuck the switch. wires. and connectors back in carefully—space can be tight.

Toggle dimmers are just a bit larger than ordinary switches. Good ones have click stops at full on and full off settings.

INSTALLING TRACK LIGHTING

Track lights might be called "unfixed fixtures." Instead of a single light source glaring mercilessly overhead, a track system lets you ring a room with soft, balanced illumination, play up a ceiling, spotlight architectural details . . . and change it all around whenever you feel like it.

Lightweight and modular, track light components assemble fairly easily. However, even a relatively modest layout may require a dozen or more different pieces. Plan carefully to know exactly how many of each you need.

The tracks themselves come in two-, four-, and eight-foot sections that can be plugged end to end to any length you like. T, X, and L couplings let you change directions, too. And with two- or three-circuit components, you can wire in separate switches to control different lights at any point along the tracks.

In plotting out an installation, you first must provide a power source. Most tracks can be fed from one end, at a coupling, or—in some cases—at any point in between. If the room already has a switch-controlled fixture, you can probably tap into its box—though that may involve fishing cable and installing a new box at the right spot, as shown on pages 21–24.

If you don't already have power up there, check with an electrician for the cost of installing a new ceiling box and wall switch. Or consider just running a switch-controlled power cord from a receptacle to the ceiling. A special adapter lets you hook in at one end of the tracks.

You also have to decide how you're going to attach the tracks to your ceiling. The drawings below show two ways to go. You also can buy special kits for attaching the track to the T-bars of a suspended ceiling or for dropping it a foot or so below a conventional ceiling.

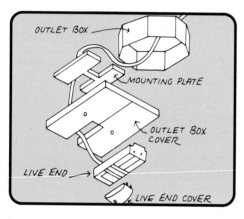

Shut off the power first, then mount a connector—either the live-end type shown here or a center feed—to the ceiling box.

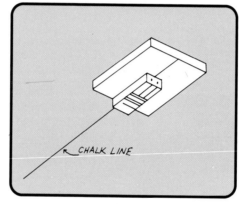

Next, snap chalk lines from the connector's center along the route you want the tracks to follow. Measure carefully.

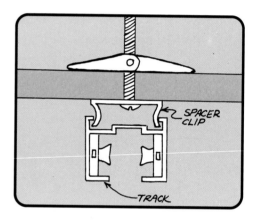

Spacer clips drop the tracks a bit so they can ride out uneven surfaces. Mount the clips first, then snap the tracks into them.

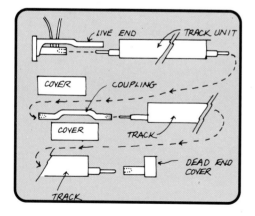

Push the couplings and tracks together as you go. Special snap-on covers give the installation a finished appearance.

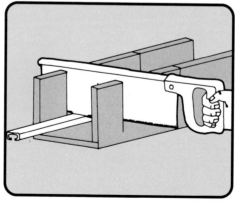

If, at the end of a run, you must cut a track, use a hacksaw and miter box. Once a unit has been cut, you can't add to it.

FLUORESCENT LIGHTING

Switching on the power to a modern-day rapid-start fluorescent light kicks off the chain reaction illustrated here. First, a *ballast* sends current to *cathodes* at either end of the tube. These excite a gas, creating barely visible *ultraviolet rays*. The rays then strike a *phosphorous coating* on the tube's inner surface, causing it to glow.

Because fluorescents don't "burn" the way incandescents do, they operate much more efficiently. A 40-watt incandescent bulb, for instance, typically produces 450 lumens—compared to over 2,000 from a 40-watt fluorescent tube.

Cooler operating temperatures help fluorescents last much longer, too. In fact, the number of times you start one—not the length of time it runs—determines the tube's life-span.

Thrifty as it is, though, fluorescent lighting has a few drawbacks. It's much less flexible than incandescent lighting because you can't interchange tubes of different wattages in the same fixture. And its illumination has a diffuse, flat quality that's ideal for task lighting, but monotonous in other situations.

You needn't, however, settle for the bluish cast that emanates from "cool white" tubes. "Warm white" and "warm white deluxe" versions more closely resemble incandescent light.

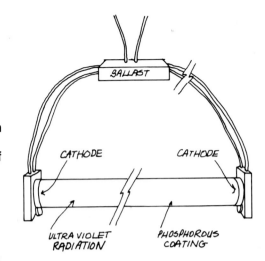

ANATOMY OF A RAPID-START FLUORESCENT LIGHT

REPLACING A STARTER

A fluorescent fixture that flickers for a few moments before lighting up probably has one additional component not shown on the anatomy above. Delayed-start fixtures preheat the cathodes with the glow from a *starter*.

When one of these goes bad (see the chart below), remove the tube, twist out the old starter, and twist in the new one (see illustration at right). Delayed-start fixtures use less electricity than rapid-start types.

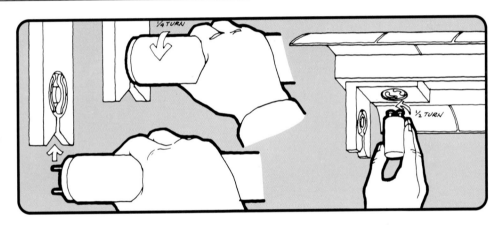

TROUBLESHOOTING FLUORESCENT LIGHTS

Problem	Causes/Solutions	
No light	It's rare for a fluorescent tube to abruptly burn out the way an incandescent bulb does, so check	electrical connections first (see page 42); replace the starter, tube, and ballast—in that order.
Partial light	If the ends light up but the center doesn't, suspect the starter. If the ends are blackening, the tube is	beginning to fail. Uniform dimming may mean that the tubes are failing or dirty.
Flickering light	Tubes often blink when they're brand new, at temperatures below 50 degrees F., and just before	they go out. If a tube blinks, it or the starter may not be properly seated.
Humming; acrid smell	These almost always indicate a ballast problem. Tighten all	ballast connections, and replace if necessary.

INSTALLING FLUORESCENT LIGHTING

To put up a fluorescent fixture, you follow essentially the same procedure shown on page 39, securing the unit to a ceiling or wall box with either a hickey or strap. You may, however, need to provide additional support, depending on the fixture's length and whether its electrical feed will be at one end or in the center. For more about this, check the drawings below.

Making the electrical connections is equally simple—you just hook the fixture's black wire to the black house wire, and the white to white.

Note, though, that most fluorescents also have a third green grounding wire. If the ceiling box has a separate ground wire, connect to this; if not, attach the ground to the box itself with a screw or special grounding clip.

If you're installing a series of fluorescent fixtures, such as you would for a room-size luminous ceiling system, plan to provide intensity controls so you can vary lighting levels to suit your needs.

The best way to do this is to connect some fixtures to one switch, others to another. Or hook them all to a single, *fluorescent-only* dimming control (ordinary dimmers just don't work with fluorescent lighting). The trouble with these, though, is that you must install a special ballast in each fixture—a costly and time-consuming proposition.

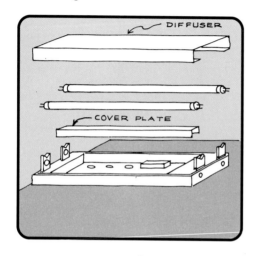

Begin by removing the diffuser, tube, and cover plate. A series of knockouts lets you bring in power from almost any direction.

For a center-feed installation, remove the center knockout and mount the unit as you would an incandescent fixture.

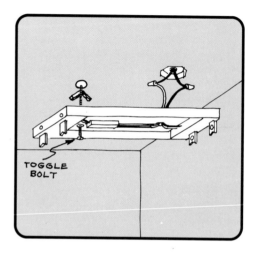

If you'll be feeding the power from one end, support the other with a screw into a joist, or a toggle bolt into the ceiling.

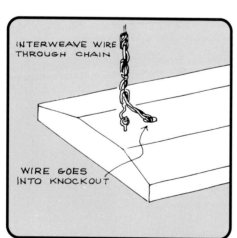

To drop a fixture closer to a work surface, suspend it with lightweight chains. Thread its wires through the links.

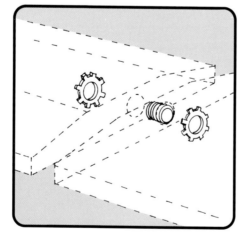

Additional knockouts and some threaded nipple couplings let you tie two or more fixtures together end to end or side to side.

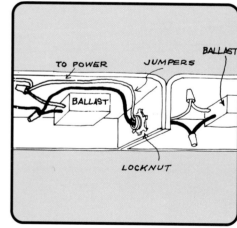

With multiple installations, you can make electrical connections within the fixtures themselves, as shown here.

H.I.D. LIGHTING

Mercury, metal halide, and sodium-vapor lights—known collectively as high intensity discharge (HID) types—combine elements of both fluorescent and incandescent lighting.

These efficient lamps use a ballast to energize the same chain of events that takes place inside a fluorescent tube (see page 41). Instead of tubes, though, HID lights feature bulbs that can be aimed almost as effectively as incandescent lights. The result: brilliant, economical illumination that can floodlight your yard, drive, or entry walk just as effectively as it does public roadways and parking lots.

HID lights vary in efficiency (see the chart below), but all put out far more light than incandescent bulbs of the same wattage—and last up to 30 times longer as well.

HID lights take three to 15 minutes to warm up, though, so don't plan to use them in frequent on/off situations. And select wattages carefully—you can't change to a bigger or smaller bulb unless you change ballasts, too.

COMPARING H.I.D. LIGHTS

Type	Properties	Uses
Mercury	Available in 50- to 1,500-watt sizes, these produce about twice as much light as an incandescent bulb of the same size. Some mercury lamps come close to matching incandescent's color quality, too.	Fixtures range from homey-looking post lanterns to no-nonsense industrial styles. Select a 50- or 75-watt lamp to illuminate a yard or driveway, and 175-watt eave lights for security.
Metal halide	Wattages range from 175 to 1,000 and are about four times as efficient as incandescent lights. Metal halide lamps cast a strong, green/white light.	These work best for floodlighting a yard or house. As with any HID type, you can control them with either a switch or an automatic light-sensitive control.
Sodium-vapor	Usually available in 250-, 400-, and 1,000-watt sizes, they're six times as efficient as incandescents, and emit the same yellow hue cast by street lights.	Where you really need a lot of light, sodium-vapor can do the job most economically. Combining these with metal halide lamps helps cool the color.

LOW-VOLTAGE LIGHTING

Low-voltage systems step down house current to a six- or 12-volt trickle, which means you can safely string together a series of fixtures like so many Christmas tree lights.

Indoors, low-voltage lets you add new fixtures almost anywhere, hooking them up with surface wiring that resembles ordinary telephone cable. You can run it easily along baseboards, window casings, and other trim.

Outdoors, low-voltage lighting is even more versatile. You simply plug a transformer into a standard 120-volt receptacle and run lightweight cable to spiked fixtures such as the one shown here. Because there's little shock hazard, you can bury the cable a few inches below ground or lay it right on the surface. Contrast this with the far more arduous job of installing underground 120-volt wiring shown on pages 32–35.

Best of all, you can alter a low-voltage layout anytime you wish—moving lights around as flowers come into bloom, for instance, or setting the stage for a patio party.

Don't, however, count on low-voltage equipment for all your outdoor lighting needs. Bulb sizes are a modest 25 and 50 watts, and don't give as much light as comparable 120-volt bulbs. For more about working with low-voltage wiring, see page 31.

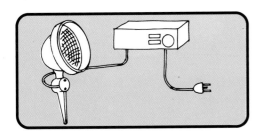

Transformers typically provide enough power to supply about 300 watts of lighting, to distances of 100 feet.

Special connectors let you snap wires to the fixtures or to each other without splicing or installing junction boxes.

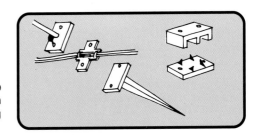

WIRING FOR SAFETY AND SECURITY

Without a doubt, secure points of entry provide the primary defense for any home. But smart homeowners don't stop there. They also take care to ensure that the lighting around the perimeter of the house is sufficient to dissuade would-be intruders . . . and that they are protected from within by one or more devices available today—electronic timers, smoke/fire detectors, and alarm systems. Incorporating any of these into your security plan will contribute significantly to the safety of everyone involved.

LIGHTING FOR SECURITY

If you ring your home with exterior lighting and use timers to orchestrate an at-home illusion, most night prowlers will shy away from your place. Yard lights can be expensive to operate, of course, so be sure to give yourself more control than just a couple of switches. This way, you can brighten only key areas most evenings. For more about exterior wiring and lighting, see pages 32–34, and 43.

Inside, you can duplicate your family's nocturnal lighting habits with one or more timing devices. You might, for example, program them to let a living room lamp burn until bedtime, then turn on a night-light. Switches on most timers let you override them when you wish. A more-expensive version controls several lights on different programs.

Moderately priced clock timers plug into an electric outlet. You plug a lamp into the timer. Keep the timer out of view.

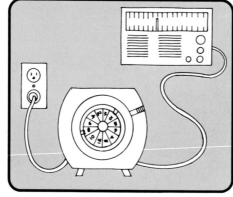

To make it sound as if someone's home during the day, program another timer to turn a radio on in the morning, off at night.

Inexpensive photoelectric cells sense darkness and turn on lights when you're away—but then leave them burning until dawn.

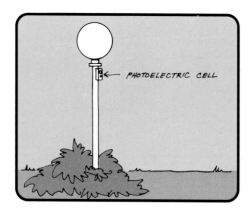

Photocells offer a good way to ensure that strategic outdoor fixtures will come on whether you're home or not.

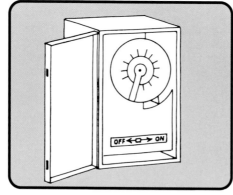

Or replace a conventional wall switch with this special timer. It turns exterior lights off as well as on at preset hours.

A pair of eave-mounted fixtures at one corner can illuminate two sides of your home. Use 40- or 60-watt bulbs here.

CHOOSING AND BUYING SMOKE DETECTORS

Even a relatively small, smoldering fire can fill a house with smoke in a matter of minutes—and smoke claims many more lives than flames. That's why fire experts strongly urge that every home be equipped with at least one smoke alarm to provide the protection you need.

In shopping for smoke detectors, you'll find two types—*photoelectric* and *ionization* units. Photoelectric types include a beam of light and a photocell. When smoke enters the unit, it scatters the light, causing part of it to contact the photocell and trigger the alarm. Slow, smoldering fires set these off more readily than fast, flaming blazes.

Ionization units employ a radioactive source that ionizes or breaks up the air inside the detector and gives it a small electrical charge. Smoke particles cut down the current flow, which sounds the warning. Ionization detectors respond more quickly than photoelectric units to fast, flaming fires.

Each type has its advantages and drawbacks. Most photoelectric models depend upon house current, which means you get no protection in a power outage or electrical fire and that you must locate them near an electric outlet. The ionization units run on house current, batteries, or both. Besides reacting more slowly to smoldering fires, they're also more susceptible to false alarms.

For greater peace of mind, consider installing at least one of each—an ionization detector in your bedroom hallway, for example, plus a photocell unit in the main living area. A truly deluxe fire protection system might also include a series of *heat sensors* wired in tandem with each other and with smoke detectors so that all the alarms will sound if just one senses excessive heat or smoke. These require extensive wiring, of course.

INSTALLING SMOKE DETECTORS

Most smoke detectors take only a few minutes to mount, and come with complete instructions. Knowing where to locate them, though, can help you decide how many you need, and might also have a bearing on the type you select.

Figure on attaching each unit to a ceiling, or high on a wall about eight to ten inches below ceiling level. Analyze your home's air currents and avoid "dead" corners with poor circulation. Also keep detectors away from smoky kitchen, furnace, garage, or fireplace areas.

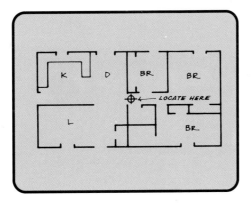

In a single-floor home with bedrooms clustered together. you probably can get by with one unit between bed and living areas.

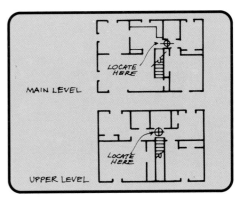

If your sleeping areas are spread out or are on different levels, you'll need at least two. Mount one at the top of the stairs.

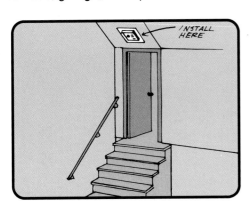

Protect your basement. too. Since smoke and heat always rise. install this detector at the top of the basement stairway. if possible.

Once smoke reaches the ceiling, it spreads out horizontally. This makes the center of the room the optimum location.

CHOOSING AND BUYING AN ALARM SYSTEM

Tripping a home alarm system sets up a din that will send almost any burglar packing. This same pandemonium also can create unpleasant headaches—for your neighbors as well as yourself—if the system frequently malfunctions or if you forget to "disarm" it.

This is why you have to weigh the high deterrent value of good security equipment against its potential for nuisance. Check community ordinances, too; some limit the loudness of an alarm device or the length of time it may sound before automatically shutting off.

If you do decide to investigate electronic security gear, you'll find dozens of different ways to go. All employ a series of *sensors* in a *network* that feeds information to a *master control.* The network may consist of lightweight, low-voltage wire strung from sensor to sensor, or it may use radio beams transmitted from sensors to a receiver in the control unit.

When a sensor tells the master control that something is awry, the control center then sets off the *reporter*—an alarm bell, siren, flashing light, automatic telephone dialer, or maybe a switchboard warning at a central-station security service. Most alarm systems include a time-delay setting so you can get out of the house and back in again without sounding the alarm. More expensive ones also may offer additional circuitry for smoke and heat detectors, and even an intercom.

Different types of sensors "feel," "hear," or "see" an intruder. *Magnetic sensors* do the feeling when a door or window opens; *pressure-sensitive mats* and metal-foil *alarm tape* are also feelers. *Ultrasonic detectors* spread inaudible sound waves to learn if anyone is moving about an area. *Infrared detectors* do the same with light beams.

Sensors, especially motion-detecting devices, can be jittery, so try to get a model with some sort of sensitivity adjustment. Also keep in mind that motion detectors can be easily set off by a night-wandering child or pet, and even certain air currents.

Installing a wired security system can be a lot of work—you have to run wire from the master control to one sensor, then the next, and so on, usually looping back to the master control at the end. Wired units cost less than radio systems, though, and with most, cutting any wire sets off the alarm.

With more-expensive radio networks, you simply install a series of battery-powered transmitters and plug in the control/receiver unit. You don't have to buy a separate transmitter for every point you want to protect; one usually will handle several nearby doors or windows. In installing one of these units, though, you do add a chore to your upkeep routine because the batteries in each transmitter must be checked periodically to make sure you don't have a "dead station."

Security system control units may be powered by stepped-down house current, batteries, or both. Batteries won't let you down in a power failure, but you should have a means of testing them—and the entire system—without activating the alarm.

ANATOMY OF A HOME ALARM SYSTEM

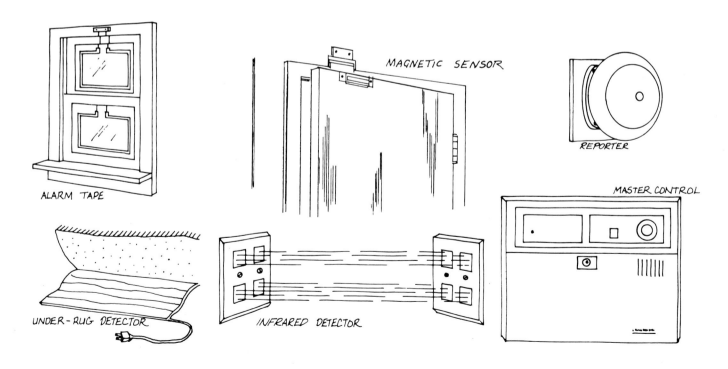

ALARM TAPE

MAGNETIC SENSOR

REPORTER

MASTER CONTROL

UNDER-RUG DETECTOR

INFRARED DETECTOR

INSTALLING AN ALARM SYSTEM

Hooking up your own security network can be an easy, one-day job or an ongoing exercise in frustration. It all depends on the care you take in installing its components.

Most problems occur at the magnetic sensors. For these devices to work properly, their two halves must always be in perfect alignment—usually with no less than 1/8 nor more than 1/4 inch between them. To maintain this tolerance, your doors and windows must fit snugly, with virtually no play. Otherwise gusts of wind or a passing truck can set off the alarm. This means you may need to tighten up doors and windows before wiring them.

Alarm circuitry varies somewhat. Most wired systems employ a *"normally closed"* circuit that keeps current moving as long as the unit is armed. Tripping or tampering with any sensor opens the circuit and sounds the alarm.

A "normally open" system—typically used with wireless setups—works the other way around. Opening a door or window *closes* the circuit. Understand which type you have, and you can better track down any problems that come up during the installation or later on.

Begin by mounting the control unit in a convenient but inconspicuous location, such as inside a closet. Next, hook up the bell or siren and test it. Then install and test each sensor before you move on to the next one. This way you know exactly where any difficulty lies.

Do-it-yourself alarm kits include only a few sensors, but you can usually add any number of additional devices. Count up all the doors and windows in your house, and you'll see that full protection could require a lot of extra hardware. To save time and expense, consider permanently fixing any windows you don't usually open—such as the upper sashes in double-hung units.

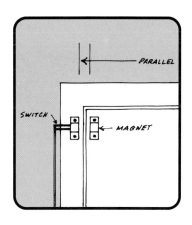

Attach each magnetic sensor's magnet to the door or window sash, its switch to the frame. These must be exactly parallel.

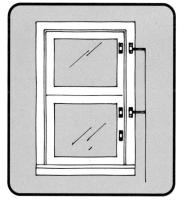

Another magnet on a double-hung sash lets you leave it part-way open—but turn off the system when you lift the window.

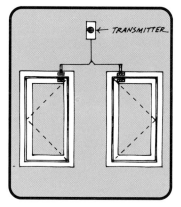

Top-mounted sensors secure casement windows. These feed into a transmitter that broadcasts to a wireless master control.

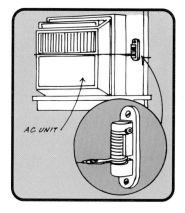

Trap switches let you string a wire across several in-swinging windows—or an air conditioner a thief might try to remove.

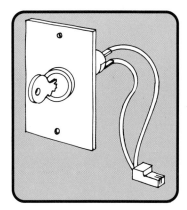

With a key switch, you can arm and disarm the system from outside. Locate this in the garage or at your back door.

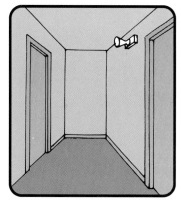

Mount an interior alarm unit in a stairway, bedroom hallway, or any other location that will widely broadcast its warning.

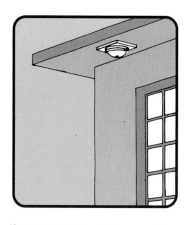

If you decide to add an outdoor bell, place it in an inaccessible spot so an intruder can't easily silence it.

INDEX

Have BETTER HOMES AND
GARDENS® magazine delivered to
your door. For information, write to:
MR. ROBERT AUSTIN
P.O. BOX 4536
DES MOINES, IA 50336